SWEET TREATS

RECIPES FROM THE

MOONGLOW CHRISTMAS SERIES

SWEET TREATS

RECIPES FROM THE
MOONGLOW CHRISTMAS SERIES

DEBORAH GARNER

CRANBERRY COVE PRESS

Cranberry Cove Press / Published by arrangement with the author

Sweet Treats: Recipes from the Moonglow Christmas Series by
Deborah Garner

Cranberry Cove Press
PO Box 1671
Jackson, WY 83001, United States

Library of Congress Catalog-in-Publication Data Available
Garner, Deborah
Sweet Treats: Recipes from the Moonglow Christmas Series /
Deborah Garner—1st United States edition
1. Non-Fiction 2. Holidays 3. Cooking

p. cm.
ISBN-13:
978-0-9969961-6-7 (paperback)

Printed in the United States of America
10 9 8 7 6 5 4 3 2 1

To the amazing readers of the Moonglow Christmas Series who share recipes for others to enjoy, and to all those who love sweet treats

Books by Deborah Garner

The Paige MacKenzie Mystery Series

Above the Bridge
The Moonglow Café
Three Silver Doves
Hutchins Creek Cache
Crazy Fox Ranch

The Moonglow Christmas Novella Series

Mistletoe at Moonglow
Silver Bells at Moonglow
Gingerbread at Moonglow
Nutcracker Sweets at Moonglow
Snowfall at Moonglow

The Sadie Kramer Flair Series

A Flair for Chardonnay
A Flair for Drama
A Flair for Beignets
A Flair for Truffles
A Flair for Flip-Flops

Cranberry Bluff

TABLE OF CONTENTS

RECIPES FROM *MISTLETOE AT MOONGLOW*   **1**

Glazed Cinnamon Nuts (A family recipe)   3
Cook's Nut Balls   4
Melting Moments   5
Ginger Crackle Cookies   6
Lemon Bars   8
Chocolate Chip Mint Cookies   9
Potato Chip Cookies   11
Chewy Coconut Cookies   12
Pumpkin Squares   13
Dark Chocolate Chunk Cookies   14
Yolanda's Chewy Oatmeal Raisin Cookies   15
Ricotta Cookies   17
Pecan Melts   18
Peanut Blossoms   19
Grandma's Shortbread Cookies   20
Holiday Eggnog Snickerdoodles   22
Spiced Apple Cookies   24
Almond Thumbprint Cookies   26
Salted Double Chocolate Chili Cookies   28
Oatmeal Chocolate Chip Cookies   30
Amish Ginger Cookies   31
Gluten Free Sugar Cookies   32
Mother's Sugar Cookies   34
Bourbon Balls   35

TABLE OF CONTENTS

RECIPES FROM *SILVER BELLS AT MOONGLOW*   **37**

Cranberry-Orange Cookies	39
Swedish Dream Cookies (Drömkakor)	41
Pecan Cookies	43
Candy Cane Brownies	44
Chocolate Chip Cherry Oatmeal Cookies	46
Thumbprint Cookies	48
Gluten-free Chocolate Chunk Cookies	49
Jumbles	51
Eggnog Cookies	53
Peppermint Candy Canes	55
Divinity Puffs	56
Snickerdoodles	57
Sharon's Chocolate Chip Cookies	59
Odessa's Pumpkin Cookies	60
Sugar Cookie Cut-Outs	61
Flourless Peanut Butter Chocolate Chip Cookies	62
Snowball Cookies	63
Grandma's Opera Fudge	65
Dutch Sour Cream Cookies	66
Soft Raisin Cookies	67
Blueberry Oatmeal Cookies	68

TABLE OF CONTENTS

RECIPES FROM *GINGERBREAD AT MOONGLOW*   **69**

Gingerbread Cookies	71
Cherry Pecan Holiday Cookies	73
Gingerbread-Eggnog Trifle	74
Homemade Eggnog	76
Cocoa Kisses	77
Lois Tallman's Ginger Snaps	78
Santa's Whiskers Cookies	79
Angel Crisp Cookies	81
Kourabiedes	82
Kitchen Sink Cookies	83
Ginger Orange Cookies	85
Christmas Swirl Fudge	87
Grandma's Kringles	89
Vegan Sugar Cookies	90
Mint Chocolate Macarons	92
Chocolate Mint Ganache Filling	95
Easy Cookies	96
Khrustyky	97
Peanut Brittle	99
Swedish Coconut Cookies	100

Table of Contents

Recipes from *Nutcracker Sweets* *at Moonglow*   **103**

Christmas Crack	105
White Christmas Fudge	107
Cathedral Cookies	108
Molasses Sugar Cookies	110
Peanut Butter Fudge	111
Lemon Crinkles	112
Krum Kake Cookies	115
Cranberry Drop Cookies	116
Double Chocolate Walnut Brownies	118
Granny's Butter Rolls	119
Christmas Hard Candy	120
Lingonberry Macarons	121
Lingonberry Buttercream Filling	124
Yummy Dates	125
Twenty-first Century Peanut Brittle	126
Healthy No-Bake Apple Energy Bites	127
Grandma Chauncey's Date Nut Bars	129
No-Bake Peanut Butter Oatmeal Cookies	130
Cinnamon Refrigerator Cookies	131
Mocha Candied Nuts	132
All-In-One-Pan Cookies	133
Date Balls	134

TABLE OF CONTENTS

RECIPES FROM *SNOWFALL* *AT MOONGLOW* **135**

Peanut Butter Cookies	137
Norwegian Kringla	138
Jo's Fudge	140
Wunderbar Ginger Bar Cookies	141
Orange Sablés	143
Lemon Nut Cookies	146
Cinnamon Cookies	147
Chocolate Peppermint Bark	148
Mrs. Prager's Cry Babies	149
Choco-Mint Puffs	150
Pecan Pie Cobbler	151
Meringue Chocolate-Chip Cookies	152
Eve's Apple Pecan Pound Cake	153
Homemade Caramel Sauce	155
Pumpkin Cookies	156
Polka Dots	157
Pfeffernüsse Fruitcake Cookies	158
Chocolate Refrigerator Cookies	160
Pecan Dreams	161
Aunt Shirley's Oatmeal Cookies	163
Lone Ranger Cookies	165
Mystery Bars	166

Recipes from *Mistletoe at Moonglow*

Excerpt from *Mistletoe at Moonglow*

Marge was the first to arrive for the cookie exchange, bringing a plate of snickerdoodles, which she placed on the buffet. Mist had heard that Marge's cookies were legendary, a town favorite. She eyed them with interest as she set out a pot of freshly brewed coffee. She'd make a point of trying them.

A few minutes later, Maisie arrived, a tub of chocolate chip mint cookies tucked under her arm. She handed Betty the container before taking off her coat, knit cap and thick, emerald green scarf and hanging them on the lobby rack.

"These look decadent, Maisie!" Betty exclaimed. "We'd better watch these carefully. We have a five-year-old chocolate fanatic running around here this year." She added the cookies to the buffet arrangement.

The variety of cookies mounted, one by one, some holiday favorites, others simply beloved family recipes. The owner of the beauty shop brought Melting Moments, a recipe she'd begged a local client for after receiving a batch as a gift one year. Soon after, Millie, the town librarian, showed up with a plate of ginger crackle cookies. She poured a cup of coffee, and joined Betty, who was in conversation with the curator of the local historical society, who had just arrived with a tin of powdered sugar concoctions.

"Cook's Nut Balls, you say?" Betty eyed the tin with delight. "I do believe I'm gaining two or three pounds every time someone walks in."

"That's what the holidays are for, Betty!" Marge laughed.

Glazed Cinnamon Nuts
(A family recipe)

Ingredients:

1 cup sugar
1/4 cup water
1/8 teaspoon cream of tartar
Heaping teaspoon of cinnamon
1 tablespoon butter
1 1/2 cups walnut halves

Directions:

Boil sugar, water, cream of tartar and cinnamon to soft ball stage (236 degrees.)

Remove from heat.

Add butter and walnuts.

Stir until walnuts separate.

Place on wax paper to cool.

COOK'S NUT BALLS
(A family recipe)

Ingredients:

1/2 cup butter
2 tablespoons sugar
1 cup flour
1 cup chopped nuts
1 teaspoon vanilla

Directions:

Mix all ingredients together and form into small balls.

Bake at 325 for 15-20 minutes.

Cool and roll in powdered sugar.

Makes about 18 cookies.

Melting Moments
(Submitted by Elisabeth Conley)

Ingredients:

1 cup brown sugar
1 cup butter
2 cups flour
Pinch of salt
1/2 teaspoon baking soda
1/2 teaspoon cream of tartar
3 teaspoons vanilla

Directions:

Cream together sugar and butter.

In separate bowl, sift together flour, salt, baking soda and cream of tartar; add to creamed mixture; add vanilla.

Drop on cookie sheet by teaspoonful.

Gently press flat with a fork dipped in milk.

Bake at 350 degrees until lightly browned, 10 minutes or less.

GINGER CRACKLE COOKIES
(Submitted by Kim McMahan Davis, from her blog, Cinnamon and Sugar and a Little Bit of Murder)

Ingredients:

2 1/4 (10 ounce) cups flour
3 teaspoons ground ginger
1 teaspoon baking soda
1 teaspoon cinnamon
1/2 teaspoon ground cloves
1/4 teaspoon salt
8 tablespoons (4 ounces) unsalted butter at room temperature
1/4 cup (2 ounces) vegetable shortening
1 cup (8 ounces) granulated sugar, plus 2/3 cup for rolling
1 large egg
1/4 cup (2 fluid ounces) molasses
1/2 to 3/4 cup crystallized ginger pieces, finely chopped

Directions:

Position oven rack to the middle. Preheat oven to 350 degrees. Line cookie sheets with parchment or Silpat.

In large bowl, combine flour, ginger, baking soda, cinnamon, cloves and salt. Whisk until well blended.

In another large bowl, combine butter, shortening and 1 cup sugar. Beat with mixer on medium-high speed until well combined. Add egg and molasses and beat until well blended. Pour in the dry ingredients and mix on low speed until well blended. Add crystallized ginger and blend in.

Pour remaining 2/3 cup sugar into shallow bowl. Using a small scoop, make 1-inch balls with dough. Roll each ball in sugar and set 2 inches apart on cookie sheets. (If dough seems too soft to work with, place in refrigerator for a couple of hours.)

Bake one sheet at a time until puffed and slightly browned around the edges, about 10 - 13 minutes. Let cool on sheet for 5 minutes, then place cookies on wire rack to cool completely.

To make ahead:

The dough can be made, shaped and rolled in sugar through step 3, then frozen for up to 2 months before baking. For best results, position the shaped dough snugly on a small cookie sheet and freeze until very firm. Then pile the frozen balls into a heavy-duty freezer bag and store in the freezer. When you're ready to bake, remove only the number of cookies you need, place them on the prepared cookie sheet and leave them on the counter while the oven heats up. Bake as directed.

Lemon Bars
(Submitted by Carol Anderson)

Ingredients:

Crust:

1 cup butter
2 cups flour
1/2 cup powdered sugar

Lemon layer:

4 eggs
4 tablespoons flour
2/3 cup lemon juice
2 cups sugar

Directions:

Cream ingredients for crust together and pat into 9 x 12 pan. Bake at 350 for 15 minutes.

Mix ingredients for lemon layer together. Pour over baked crust.

Bake at 350 for 20 minutes.

Cool. Sprinkle with powdered sugar. Cut into squares.

Chocolate Chip Mint Cookies

(Submitted by Beth Britain, originally from Mollie Katzen's "Still Life with Menu")

Ingredients:

3/4 cup (1 1/2 sticks) butter
1/2 cup packed brown sugar
1/2 cup granulated sugar
1 egg
1 teaspoon vanilla extract
1 teaspoon peppermint extract
1 1/2 cups unbleached white flour
1/4 cup unsweetened cocoa
1 teaspoon baking soda
1/4 teaspoon salt
1 cup chocolate chips

Directions:

Preheat oven to 350 degrees.

Lightly grease a cookie sheet.

Cream together butter and sugars with an electric mixer at high speed. Beat in egg. Stir in vanilla and peppermint extracts.

Sift together dry ingredients and add them to the butter mixture along with the chocolate chips. Stir until well combined.

Drop by rounded teaspoons onto a lightly greased cookie sheet.

Bake at 350 for 12-15 minutes.

Remove from sheet immediately after baking and cool on a wire rack.

POTATO CHIP COOKIES
(Submitted by Erika Bonham Kehlet)

Start with:

1 cup butter
1/2 cup sugar
1 teaspoon vanilla

Cream above ingredients together.

Add:

1/2 cup crushed potato chips
1/2 cup chopped pecans
2 cups flour

Roll into walnut sized balls.

Flatten with a glass dipped in granulated sugar.

Place on ungreased cookie sheet.

Bake at 350 degrees for 12-15 minutes.

CHEWY COCONUT COOKIES
(Submitted by Valerie Peterson)

Ingredients:

2 cups sugar
1 cup shortening
2 eggs
1 teaspoon salt
1 teaspoon soda
1 teaspoon vanilla
2 cups flour
2 cups oatmeal
1 1/2 cups ground raisins
1/2 cup coconut

Directions:

Cream together sugar and shortening.

Add eggs, salt, soda and vanilla. Beat well.

Add flour, oatmeal and raisins. Add coconut last.

Roll in balls the size of a walnut.

Place on cookie sheet and bake at 375 degrees for 12 minutes.

Pumpkin Squares
(Submitted by Carol Ann Kauffman)

Crust:

1 cup flour	1/2 cup brown sugar
1/2 cup rolled oats	1/2 cup melted butter

Mix together. Spread on bottom of 9 x 13 pan. Bake 15 minutes at 350 degrees. Cool.

Filling:

1 pound can pumpkin	1/2 teaspoon cinnamon
1 can evaporated milk	1 teaspoon pumpkin pie
2 eggs	spice
3/4 cup sugar	Pinch of nutmeg
1/2 teaspoon salt	

Mix. Pour over crust. Bake 20 minutes at 350 degrees.

Topping:

3/4 cup walnut
1/2 cup brown sugar
2 tablespoons melted butter

Mix and spread on top of cooked pumpkin mix. Put back in oven for another 15 minutes.

Note: Double recipe for a cookie sheet size.

DARK CHOCOLATE CHUNK COOKIES

(Submitted by S.A. Molteni, author of I.T. Geek to Farm Girl Freak)

Ingredients:

1 cup butter (2 sticks)	1 1/2 teaspoons vanilla
1/2 cup granulated sugar	2 1/2 cups all-purpose
1 cup packed brown sugar	flour
1/2 teaspoon baking soda	1 giant Hershey's Dark
1/2 teaspoon salt	Chocolate Bar chopped
2 eggs	into chunks

Directions:

In a large mixing bowl, beat the butter with an electric mixer on medium to high speed for 30 seconds. Add brown sugar, granulated sugar, salt and baking soda. Beat mixture until combined. Add in the eggs and vanilla, beat until well blended. Beat in half of the flour, and then stir in remaining flour. Stir in chocolate pieces.

Drop dough by rounded teaspoons on an ungreased cookie sheet.

Bake at 350 degrees for 9-11 minutes or until edges are lightly browned.

Transfer cookies to a wire rack or wax paper and let cool.

Makes about 48 cookies.

Yolanda's Chewy Oatmeal Raisin Cookies

(Submitted by Lisa Maliga, author of The Aroma of Love, from The Yolanda's Yummery Series, Book 3)

Ingredients:

1 cup unsalted butter, softened to room temperature
1 cup dark brown sugar
1/4 cup granulated sugar
2 large eggs (room temperature)
2 teaspoons vanilla extract
1 1/2 cups all-purpose flour
1 teaspoon baking soda
1 1/2 teaspoons ground cinnamon
1/2 teaspoon salt
3 cups rolled oats
1 1/2 cups raisins
1 cup chopped walnuts (optional)

Directions:

In a medium bowl, add the butter, brown sugar and white sugar. Mix on low to medium speed until creamy.

Add eggs and mix well. With a spatula, scrape the sides, and then add the vanilla extract. Mix well until combined.

In a larger bowl, mix the flour, baking soda, cinnamon and salt together. Add to the wet ingredients, and mix on low until combined.

Beat in the oats and raisins on low speed. Add the walnuts last.

For puffier cookies, refrigerate the dough for one hour.

Preheat oven to 350 degrees. Line two large baking sheets with parchment paper.

Using a standard tablespoon, scoop dough and place 2 inches apart on baking sheets. Bake for 10 minutes until lightly browned on the sides. The centers will look very soft and lighter in color.

Remove from the oven and let cool on baking sheet for 5 minutes before transferring to a wire rack to cool completely.

RICOTTA COOKIES

(Submitted by Lia Garret)

Ingredients:

2 cups all-purpose flour
1/2 teaspoon salt
1 tablespoon baking powder
1 cup sugar
1/2 cup butter, softened
1 8 ounce container ricotta cheese
1 teaspoon vanilla extract
1 large egg
1/4 to 1/2 teaspoon orange or lemon oil (optional)
Colored sprinkles (optional)

Directions:

Preheat oven to 350 degrees.
Mix flour, salt and baking powder together.

Cream butter and sugar together until light and fluffy.

Add ricotta, vanilla, egg and orange oil, mix well.
Stir in dry ingredients.

Drop by tablespoon on ungreased cookie sheet. If using sprinkles, add sprinkles before baking.

Bake about 15 minutes, until edges are very light brown.

Makes about 36 cookies.

PECAN MELTS

(Submitted by Valerie Peterson)

Ingredients:

1/2 cup butter
1/3 cup sugar
1 egg (unbeaten)
1 cup flour
1/2 teaspoon salt
2 tablespoons orange juice
1/2 teaspoon grated orange rind
3/4 cup chopped pecans

Directions:

Cream together butter and sugar.

Blend in unbeaten egg.

Add half of the flour and salt.

Add orange juice and remaining flour and salt

Add grated orange rind. Stir in pecans.

Drop on cookie sheet by rounded teaspoons and bake at 350 degrees for 9-12 minutes.

Roll in powdered sugar while hot.

PEANUT BLOSSOMS
(Submitted by Carol Anderson)

Ingredients:

1 1/2 cups flour
1 teaspoon soda
1/2 teaspoon salt
1/2 cup sugar
1/2 cup brown sugar, packed
1/2 cup shortening or butter
1/2 cup smooth peanut butter
1 egg
2 tablespoons milk
1 teaspoon vanilla
Approx. 48 chocolate kisses (foil removed)
Additional granulated sugar for rolling

Directions:

Place all ingredients, except kisses, in a mixing bowl and stir until dough forms. Shape dough into balls about the size of walnuts. Roll balls in additional sugar and place on cookie sheet 2 inches apart.

Bake at 375 degrees for 10 minutes. Top each cookie immediately with a kiss. Press down firmly so cookie cracks around the edge.

GRANDMA'S SHORTBREAD COOKIES
(Submitted by Debbie Brown)

Cook Time: 15 to 20 min.

Ingredients:

1/2 cup (125 ml) cornstarch
1/2 cup (125 ml) icing sugar
1 cup (250 ml) all-purpose flour
3/4 cup (175 ml) butter, softened

Directions:

Sift together cornstarch, sugar and flour. With wooden spoon, blend in butter until a soft, smooth dough forms.

Shape into 1-inch (2.5 cm) balls. If dough is too soft to handle, cover and chill for 30 to 60 minutes. Place 1 1/2 inches (4 cm) apart on ungreased baking sheets; flatten with lightly floured fork. Alternatively, roll dough to 1/4 inch (6 mm); cut into shapes with cookie cutters. Decorate with candied cherries, colored sprinkles or nuts, if desired.

Bake at 300 degrees (150 degrees C) for 15 to 20 minutes or until edges are lightly browned. Cool on wire rack.

To make crescents, add 1/2 cup (125 ml) ground almonds or hazelnuts to flour mixture. Shape into logs about 1/2 inch (1 cm) thick and 3 inches (7 cm) long. Curve into crescent shapes. When baked and cool, dip ends in melted chocolate.

Makes around 24 cookies.

HOLIDAY EGGNOG SNICKERDOODLES
(Submitted by Diane Peterson)

Ingredients:

1/2 cup butter, softened
1/2 cup shortening
2 cups plus 1/3 cup sugar, divided
1 egg
1 teaspoon rum extract
1/2 cup evaporate milk
1/2 cup refrigerated French Vanilla nondairy creamer
5 1/2 cups all-purpose flour
1 teaspoon salt
1 teaspoon baking soda
1/2 teaspoon ground nutmeg

ICING:

1 cup powdered sugar
5-6 teaspoons French Vanilla creamer

Directions:

Preheat oven to 350 degrees. In large bowl, cream butter, shortening, and 2 cups sugar until light and fluffy. Beat in egg and extract.

In small bowl, mix milk and creamer.
In another bowl, whisk flour, salt and baking soda; gradually add to creamed mixture alternately with milk mix, beating well after each addition.

In a small bowl, mix nutmeg and remaining sugar. Shape dough into 1 inch balls; roll in nutmeg mix.

Place 2 inches apart on ungreased baking sheets; flatten slightly with bottom of glass.

Bake 10-12 minutes or until lightly browned. Cool on baking sheets for 2 minutes. Remove to wire racks, cool completely.

For icing: mix powdered sugar and creamer to reach desired consistency. Pipe snowflake designs on cookies.

Makes about 7 1/2 dozen cookies.

SPICED APPLE COOKIES
(Submitted by Valerie Peterson)

Ingredients:

1 cup raisins
1/2 cup shortening
1 1/3 cups packed brown sugar
1 egg
1/4 cup milk
2 1/4 cups all-purpose flour
1 teaspoon baking soda
1 teaspoon ground cinnamon
1/2 teaspoon salt
1/2 teaspoon cloves
1/2 teaspoon nutmeg
1 cup chopped walnuts
1 cup chopped unpeeled apple

Directions:

In small saucepan, cover raisins with water. Bring to boil, remove from heat. Cover and let stand for 5 minutes. Drain.

Meanwhile, in large mixing bowl, beat together shortening and brown sugar. Beat in egg and milk.

Stir together flour, soda, cinnamon, salt, cloves and nutmeg. Add to shortening mixture. Beat until well-blended.

Stir in nuts, apple and drained raisins.

Drop by rounded teaspoons on ungreased cookie sheet and bake at 375 degrees for 8 minutes. Immediately remove from cookie sheet and cool on wire rack.

Makes about 3 dozen medium cookies.

ALMOND THUMBPRINT COOKIES
(Submitted by Debbie Brown)

Ingredients:

3/4 cup butter, softened
2/3 cup granulated sugar
2 eggs
1 1/4 cups ground almonds
2 cups baking flour
1/2 teaspoon ground cinnamon
1/2 teaspoon salt
1/2 cup apricot or peach jam

Directions:

Grease rimless baking sheets or line with parchment paper; set aside.

In a large bowl, beat butter with sugar until fluffy. Separate 1 of the eggs; drop white into a small shallow bowl and set aside. Add yolk and remaining egg to butter mixture; beat well.

In a separate bowl, whisk together 1/3 cup of the almonds, flour, cinnamon and salt; add to butter mixture in 2 additions and stir just until blended.

Lightly beat reserved egg white with 1 tablespoon water. Place remaining almonds in a shallow dish.

Roll dough by scant 1 tablespoon into balls. Dip each into egg white mixture; roll in almonds to coat. Place 2 inches apart on prepared pans. Using end of wooden spoon, make an indent in the center of each.

Bake in top and bottom thirds of 350 degree oven, rotating and switching pans halfway through until light golden, about 15 minutes. Press indent again. Transfer to wire rack; let cool. Fill indent with jam of choice. Or, before baking, press an unblanched almond into the cookie instead of making an indentation.

Makes about 35 cookies.

To make ahead: Layer between waxed paper in airtight container, and store for up to 2 days or freeze for up to 3 weeks.

SALTED DOUBLE CHOCOLATE CHILI COOKIES

(Submitted by Kim McMahan Davis, from her blog, Cinnamon and Sugar and a Little Bit of Murder)

Ingredients:

1 1/3 cups all-purpose flour
2 tablespoons cornstarch
1 cup Dutch-processed cocoa powder
1 1/2 teaspoons flaky sea salt or kosher salt
3/4 teaspoon baking soda
3/4 teaspoon baking powder
1/2 to 1 teaspoon cayenne powder
3/4 cup unsalted butter, room temperature
1 cup packed brown sugar
3/4 cup granulated sugar
2 teaspoons pure vanilla extract
2 eggs, room temperature
1 1/2 cups semi-sweet or dark chocolate chips
Additional granulated sugar for rolling

Directions:

Preheat oven to 350 degrees.

Whisk the flour, cornstarch, cocoa powder, salt, baking soda, baking powder and cayenne powder together in a bowl. Set aside.

In a stand mixer fitted with the paddle attachment, cream butter until pale and fluffy, about 2 minutes, scraping down bowl as needed. Beat in sugars until smooth and fluffy again.

On low, add in vanilla and one egg at a time, scraping as needed, until incorporated.

Add in half the flour mixture on low and mix to incorporate before adding the other half.

Mix the flour in until just incorporated. Stir in the chocolate chips with a wooden spoon.

Refrigerate the dough for 12-24 hours, freeze the dough for about 1 hour, or bake the cookies straight away. There is less spread with chilled dough.

Roll the dough into tablespoon-sized balls and then roll in granulated sugar.

Place them about 2 inches apart on a parchment lined baking sheet.

Bake 10-12 minutes. Let cool briefly and then remove to a wire rack to finish cooling.

Makes about 32-40 cookies

OATMEAL CHOCOLATE CHIP COOKIES
(Submitted by Valerie Peterson)

Ingredients:

1 cup margarine
1 cup brown sugar
1 cup white sugar
2 eggs
2 cups flour
1 teaspoon baking soda
1/2 teaspoon salt
1/2 teaspoon baking powder
1 teaspoon vanilla
2 cups oatmeal
1 package chocolate chips

Directions:

Mix all ingredients in the order given.

Place by teaspoon on ungreased cookie sheet.

Bake at 350 degrees for about 10 minutes.

AMISH GINGER COOKIES
(Submitted by Debbie Brown)

Ingredients:

3/4 cup butter, softened
1 cup granulated sugar
1 egg
1/4 cup unsulfured molasses
2 1/2 cups all-purpose flour
1 teaspoon ground ginger
1 teaspoon ground cloves
1 teaspoon ground cinnamon
1 1/2 teaspoons baking soda
Additional granulated sugar for rolling

Directions:

Preheat oven to 350 degrees.

In a mixing bowl, beat together butter and 1 cup sugar until creamy. Add egg and molasses; beat until combined. Add the remaining ingredients and mix until well combined.

Roll dough into 1-inch balls and roll in the extra granulated sugar.

Place balls on ungreased baking sheet. Bake for 5 - 7 minutes until barely turning brown. Cool for 1 minute on baking sheet and then remove to wire racks to cool completely.

Makes about 48 cookies.

GLUTEN FREE SUGAR COOKIES
(Submitted by Debbie Brown)

Ingredients:

1 1/2 cups white rice flour
1/2 teaspoon cream of tartar
1 1/2 teaspoons xanthan gum
1/2 teaspoon baking soda
1/8 teaspoon salt
1/2 cup butter or margarine
1 egg
1/2 teaspoon gluten free vanilla, lemon, or almond flavoring
1/2 cup sugar

Directions:

Preheat the oven to 350 degrees.

Mix the first 5 ingredients in a bowl. Once they are well combined, add the butter and mix together until ingredients become crumbly.

In a separate bowl combine the egg, flavoring and sugar and use a whisker to combine. Add this mixture to the dry ingredients. Mix it all until it recedes from the sides.

Shape the dough into a flat circle. Chill in the refrigerator for about an hour. Place the dough on freezer paper sprinkled with gluten free flour. You can substitute powdered sugar for the flour.

Roll out to 1/4 inch thickness, then cut with cookie cutters.

Place cookies on a lightly greased cookie sheet and bake for 12 minutes. Remove from oven when done and cool on wire rack.

Makes about 20 cookies.

MOTHER'S SUGAR COOKIES
(Submitted by Barb Goss)

Ingredients:

6 cups flour
4 sticks margarine
2 cups sugar
4 eggs
4 teaspoons baking
powder

2 teaspoons salt
1 cup milk
1 teaspoon vanilla
2 tablespoons anise seeds
(or 3 tablespoons anise
extract)

Directions:

Mix sugar, eggs and margarine.

Add milk.

Mix dry ingredients and combine gradually.

Roll out dough and cut with cookie cutters.

Bake at 350 degrees for 8-10 minutes.

*** Add more flour if necessary for firm batter.

*** Depending on egg size, you may need 7 cups of flour.

*** Thicker cut will be more cake-like, thinner cut will be crisper.

Bourbon Balls

(Submitted by Vicky Kaseorg)

Ingredients:

1 package vanilla wafers, roughly ground
1 cup chopped walnuts
3 tablespoons corn syrup
1/2 cup bourbon
Powdered sugar

Directions:

Put one bag of vanilla wafers in food processor until roughly ground. Add walnuts.

Process into rice-sized pieces. Pour in bowl.

Add 3 tablespoons corn syrup.

Add 1/2 cup bourbon (or to taste.)

Roll in palms to form 1-inch balls.

Roll in powdered sugar.

Cover and chill or freeze up to one month.

Recipes From
Silver Bells at Moonglow

Excerpt from *Silver Bells at Moonglow*

Mist turned to the small refrigerated display. "Definitely some of the white roses. Those will add elegance to the hydrangeas and lilies. I'll pass on the red ones, but I'll take as many of those white button chrysanthemums as you can give me, as well as red berries, spruce, and eucalyptus to work inside the arrangements."

"You need any pinecones, branches, or that type of thing?" Maisie pulled the roses and chrysanthemums from the cooler and wrapped them in paper.

"I saved all the nonperishable decorations from last year," Mist said. "I've been using many in fall arrangements but will rework them all into Christmas displays tonight. We only have one guest arriving this evening. The rest come in tomorrow."

"Betty's annual cookie exchange is tomorrow too, isn't it?"

"Yes, it is," Mist said. "Making this one busy weekend."

"Ooh, count me in on that. I already know I'm bringing snickerdoodles. I'll just have to hide them so they don't disappear before the exchange."

Mist laughed. "Yes, I imagine there will be plenty of hidden cookies around town." She gathered four huge paper bundles into her arms and rested them against her right shoulder, craning her neck around them to bid good-bye to Maisie. "See you at the cookie exchange, if not before. Thank you for bringing in such beautiful ingredients this year."

"Ingredients?" Maisie said, a quizzical expression on her face. "Are you getting confused with the talk about baking?"

"Not at all, Maisie," Mist said, smiling. "Everything is an ingredient of something else. These flowers are ingredients for holiday memories, just like flour and sugar."

CRANBERRY-ORANGE COOKIES
(Submitted by Kim McMahan Davis, from her blog, Cinnamon and Sugar and a Little Bit of Murder)

Makes approximately 45 small cookies

Ingredients:

3/4 cup (4.7 ounces) dried cranberries
3/4 cup (5.3 ounces) granulated sugar
2 cups (9 ounces) all-purpose flour
1-1/2 teaspoons baking powder
1/2 teaspoon salt
1/2 cup (4 ounces) cold butter, cut into small pieces
1 egg, lightly beaten
1/4 cup orange juice
1/4 teaspoon orange extract
1/2 teaspoon red gel food coloring (optional)
Red and white coarse sugar, for rolling

Directions:

Using a food processor, pulse the dried cranberries and sugar together until the cranberries are finely ground.

Add the flour, baking powder, and salt. Pulse to combine.

Add the cold butter pieces and pulse to incorporate, until the mixture is the size of small peas. This can take about 20 pulses.

Whisk the orange juice, egg, orange extract, and food coloring (if using) in a small bowl.

Drizzle the orange juice mixture over the flour mixture in the food processor and pulse until a dough forms.

Place the dough in a bowl and cover tightly with plastic wrap. Refrigerate for at least 1 hour.

Preheat the oven to 350°F.

Place 1/4 cup red coarse sugar and 1/4 cup white coarse sugar in a shallow bowl and mix. Set aside.

Scoop the cookie dough into 1-inch to 1-1/2-inch balls, then roll in the coarse sugar mixture. Place the sugar-coated dough on a parchment-lined baking sheet, 12 cookies to each sheet.

Bake 12 to 16 minutes or until the tops of the cookies are just set and the bottom of the cookies are barely golden. Remove from the oven and cool for 5 minutes on the baking sheet, then transfer to a wire rack to cool completely. Store in an airtight container for up to 5 days.

SWEDISH DREAM COOKIES (DRÖMKAKOR)
(Submitted by Kathy Tucker)

Called dream cookies because they are light and airy, these melt in your mouth

Makes 40-45 cookies

Ingredients:

1 2/3 cups flour
1 teaspoon baking soda
1 1/4 cups sugar
8 tablespoons, unsalted butter, softened (1 stick)
1 1/4 cups sugar
1 tablespoon vanilla sugar
1/3 cup corn oil

Directions:

Heat oven to 300°F. In a small bowl, whisk together flour and baking soda; set aside. In a large bowl and using a handheld mixer on medium speed, beat butter and sugars until pale and fluffy, 1-2 minutes. Add oil and mix until smooth. Add dry ingredients and stir until just combined.

Using a tablespoon-size measuring spoon, divide dough into about 40 portions. Using your hands, shape the dough portions into balls 2 inches apart on baking sheets lined with parchment paper.

Bake 1 sheet at a time until cookies crack on top and are just set, 25-30 minutes.

Transfer to a wire rack and let cool before serving.

PECAN COOKIES
(Submitted by Jan Harvey)

Ingredients:

2 cups butter (4 sticks)
1/2 cup sugar
4 scant cups of flour
1 1/2 cups chopped pecans

Directions:

Combine all ingredients and roll into balls the size of a walnut. Bake at 375°F for 15-20 minutes. While cookies are warm – roll in powdered sugar.

CANDY CANE BROWNIES
(Submitted by Kim McMahan Davis, from her blog,
Cinnamon and Sugar and a Little Bit of Murder)

Ingredients:

Brownies
3 sticks (1-1/2 cups)
butter
3 cups sugar
5 eggs
1 teaspoon salt

3/4 teaspoon peppermint
extract
3/4 cup cocoa powder
2-1/4 cups all-purpose
flour

Frosting

4 tablespoons butter
2 cups confectioners' sugar
2 tablespoons heavy whipping cream
1/2 teaspoon peppermint extract

Garnish
Coarsely broken candy canes

Directions:

Brownies
Preheat oven to 350°F.

Whisk flour with the cocoa powder and set aside.

Cream butter and sugar with an electric mixer.

Beat in eggs, one at a time.

Add salt and peppermint extract and mix well.

Gradually add in the cocoa and flour mixture and stir until completed incorporated.

Line a jelly roll pan (15-1/2"x10-1/2"x1") with parchment paper. Spritz the parchment paper with non-stick cooking spray. Spread the batter evenly in the prepared pan.

Bake for about 30 minutes or until a wooden skewer inserted in the middle comes out clean. Rest pan on a wire rack until completely cool before proceeding with frosting.

Frosting
Mix the butter and confectioners' sugar together until butter is incorporated completely. Add the heavy whipping cream, 1 tablespoon at a time, whipping well after each addition. Add the peppermint extract and whip for an additional 2 minutes.

Frost the brownies then cut into 2-inch squares. Garnish each square with bits of broken candy canes right before serving.

CHOCOLATE CHIP CHERRY OATMEAL COOKIES

(Submitted by Sue Doucette)

Ingredients:

3/4 cup good semisweet chocolate chips
3/4 cup chopped dried sweet cherries
1 teaspoon finely grated orange zest
1 teaspoon vanilla
1/4 cup water
1 cup brown sugar
3/4 cup shortening or butter
1/2 granulated sugar
1 egg
3 cups uncooked oatmeal or quick oatmeal (don't use steel cut)
1 cup flour
1 teaspoon salt
1/2 teaspoon baking soda

Directions:

Heat oven to 350°F.

Beat brown sugar, sugar, shortening or butter. Add water, beaten egg and vanilla.

Add dry ingredients and orange zest and mix into the above mixture in small batches. Fold in chocolate chips and cherries.

Use a small ice cream scoop to scoop equal sized cookie dough balls and place on an ungreased cookie sheet.

Bake 12-15 minutes depending upon size of scoop.

Cool on a cooling rack and enjoy.

Option: substitute a little cinnamon for the orange zest.

THUMBPRINT COOKIES
(Submitted by Jan Harvey)

Ingredients:

1/2 cup shortening
1/2 cup butter
1 egg yolk (save white)
1/2 teaspoon vanilla
1 cup sifted flour
1/4 teaspoon salt
Chopped walnuts

Directions:

Mix together shortening, butter, egg yolk and vanilla.

Sift together flour and salt. Stir into shortening mixture.

Roll into 1 inch balls. Dip in slightly beaten egg white. Roll in finely chopped walnuts.

Place 1 inch apart on ungreased cookie sheet. Bake 5 minutes at 375°F.

Remove from oven and place a candy cherry in center. Return to oven and bake 8 minutes longer. Cool.

Gluten-free Chocolate Chunk Cookies

(Submitted by Kim McMahan Davis, from her blog, Cinnamon and Sugar and a Little Bit of Murder)

These cookies use whole grain flour, to boost the nutritional value...but they're still delicious and make a satisfying dessert! Buckwheat is a gluten-free grain, despite its name. If you prefer, you can use brown rice flour instead, or if gluten is not an issue, substitute equal amounts of white whole-wheat flour.

Ingredients:

1 cup (7.5 ounces) packed brown sugar
1/3 cup canola oil
1/3 cup butter, room temperature
2 tablespoons honey
1-1/2 teaspoons vanilla extract (make sure to use a gluten-free brand if necessary, or omit)
1 large egg, room temperature
2 cups (9 ounces) Buckwheat flour (use the lightly spoon and level method if not using a scale)
1 teaspoon baking soda
1/2 teaspoon salt
4 ounces premium semisweet or bittersweet chocolate, chopped
1/2 teaspoon Fleur de sel or other coarse sea salt (optional)

Directions:

Preheat oven to 375°F.

Add brown sugar, canola oil, butter, honey, and vanilla extract to the bowl of a standing mixer. Beat on medium until well combined.

Add the egg and beat until thoroughly incorporated.

Whisk together the flour, baking soda, and salt.

Add the flour mixture to the sugar mixture and beat on low speed until blended together.

Add the chocolate and mix by hand until just incorporated.

Place rounded tablespoon-sized pieces of cookie dough on a parchment-lined baking sheet. Sprinkle a bit of the Fleur de sel over each cookie, if desired.

Bake 8 to 11 minutes until the edges start to brown. Remove the baking sheet from the oven and allow the cookies to cool on the sheet for 5 minutes, then place them on a wire rack to cool completely. Store in an airtight container in a cool, dry place.

Makes about 24 cookies, depending on size.

JUMBLES
(Submitted by Linda Smith)

Ingredients:

3/4 cup pecan halves
1 1/4 cups whole almonds
1/2 cup sugar
1/4 cup brown sugar
8 tablespoons (1 stick) butter
1 egg
3/4 teaspoon vanilla
1 cup + 2 tablespoon flour
1 teaspoon baking soda
1/4 teaspoon salt
1 cup semisweet chocolate chips
1 1/2 cups raisins

Directions:

Preheat oven to 375°F.

Place the nuts on cookie sheet. Bake them, stirring occasionally, for about 7 minutes or until they begin to have a toasted aroma. Do not bake until the almond skins begin to crack. Cool completely. Chop into very coarse pieces.

Cream the sugars and butter until light and fluffy. Beat in the egg and vanilla until well blended. Sift the flour, baking soda and salt. On low speed, beat in the flour mixture until incorporated.

In a large bowl, stir together the chocolate chips, raisins, pecans and almonds. Empty the batter into the bowl and mix together evenly with a large spoon or spatula.

Drop batter by rounded teaspoons onto the cookie sheets. Bake for 12-15 minutes or until golden brown – will still be somewhat soft inside.

EGGNOG COOKIES

(Submitted by Frances Hampton)

Ingredients:

3 1/2 cups all-purpose flour
1/2 teaspoon baking soda
1/2 teaspoon ground nutmeg
1/2 teaspoon salt
16 tablespoons unsalted butter (2 sticks) *softened on counter 1 hour
3/4 cup granulated sugar
1/4 cup light brown sugar, packed
1 large egg
1/2 cup eggnog

Eggnog Glaze

2 cups powdered sugar (for thicker glaze use 2 1/2 cups)
2 tablespoons clear vanilla extract (this makes the glaze white and not brownish white if using regular vanilla extract.)
3 tablespoons eggnog

Directions:

In a large bowl, sift together the flour, baking soda, nutmeg, and salt.

Using a mixer, beat softened butter, granulated sugar, and brown sugar on medium-high speed until fluffy, about 2 minutes. Add egg and beat until combined. Reduce speed to low, add flour mixture, and mix until combined. Do not overmix!

Add eggnog and mix 3 times with a spatula, until combined. Do not overmix!

Divide dough into 4 pieces, wrap in plastic wrap, and refrigerate for at least 1 hour.

Preheat oven to 375ºF. Line two large baking sheets with parchment paper or silicone baking mats. Set aside.

In a medium sized bowl, whisk together powdered sugar, vanilla extract, and eggnog until smooth. Set aside.
Roll out dough to about 1/8 inch thick. Using a cookie cutter, cut dough into shapes.

Place cookie shapes onto prepared baking pan. Bake for 8-10 minutes. Let cookies cool on baking sheet for 10 minutes, then transfer to wire rack. Let cookies cool completely before icing and decorating. Once cookies are cooled, dip cookies into glaze and sprinkle with colored sprinkles. Place cookies on baking sheet to set for at least 30 minutes before serving. To speed up the setting time, place cookies in the fridge for about 10-15 minutes.

PEPPERMINT CANDY CANES
(Submitted by Jan Harvey)

Ingredients:

1/2 cup shortening
1/2 cup sugar
1 egg yolk
1 1/2 teaspoon vanilla
1 1/2 cups sifted enriched flour
1/2 teaspoon baking powder
1/4 teaspoon salt
3 tablespoons milk
3/4 teaspoon peppermint extract
Red food coloring

Directions:

Preheat oven to 375°F.

Cream shortening and sugar. Blend in egg yolk and vanilla. Sift dry ingredients; add alternately with milk. Add peppermint extract: mix well.

Add red food coloring to 1/2 of dough. Chill. Shape into candy canes with alternate red and white cookie dough and shape into 5 inch rolled strips. Twist into canes.

Bake at 375°F for about 10 minutes.

DIVINITY PUFFS
(Submitted by Valerie Peterson)

Ingredients:

2 cups white sugar
1/2 cup light corn syrup
1/2 cup water
Dash of salt
2 stiffly beaten egg whites
1 teaspoon vanilla extract

Directions:

Stir sugar into syrup, water and salt. Cook to dissolve sugar. Then boil to 240°F. Slowly pour 1/3rd of syrup over stiffly beaten egg whites, stirring constantly. Cook remaining syrup to a hard-boiled stage 265°. Beat into egg white mixture. Continue beating. When mixture holds shape, add vanilla. Drop from teaspoon on waxed paper.

SNICKERDOODLES
(Submitted by Peggy Hyndman)

Ingredients:

1 cup butter (2 sticks)
1-1/2 cups sugar
2 large eggs
2 3/4 cups flour
2 teaspoons cream of tartar
1 teaspoon baking soda
1/4 teaspoon salt
3 tablespoons sugar
3 teaspoons cinnamon

Directions:

Mix butter, 1 1/2 cups sugar and eggs thoroughly in a large bowl.

Combine flour, cream of tartar, baking soda and salt in a separate bowl. Blend dry ingredients into butter mixture.

Chill dough, and chill an ungreased cookie sheet for about 10-15 minutes in the fridge.

Meanwhile, mix 3 tablespoons sugar, and 3 teaspoons cinnamon in a small bowl.
Scoop 1 inch balls of dough into the sugar/ cinnamon mixture.

Coat by gently rolling balls of dough in the sugar mixture.

Place on chilled ungreased cookie sheet, and bake 10 minutes at 375°F.

Remove from pan immediately.

SHARON'S CHOCOLATE CHIP COOKIES
(Submitted by Sharon Guagliardo)

Ingredients:

1 cup butter
3/4 cup sugar
1/2 cup brown sugar
2 eggs
2 teaspoons vanilla
2 1/4 cup flour
1/2 teaspoon baking soda
1 teaspoon salt
1 package chocolate chips
1/2 cup chopped walnuts

Directions:

Cream butter and sugars. Add eggs and vanilla. Mix the remaining dry ingredients together. Hand mix all ingredients together. Drop by rounded tablespoonful on ungreased cookies sheet and bake at 375°F for 8 to 10 minutes. Makes about 3 dozen 2 inch cookies, or about 4 dozen 1 1/2 inch cookies.

ODESSA'S PUMPKIN COOKIES
(Submitted by Odessa Green)

Ingredients:

2 3/4 cups all-purpose
flour
1 tsp baking soda
1 tsp baking powder
1 tsp cinnamon
1/2 tsp nutmeg
1/2 tsp ginger
1/2 tsp salt

1 stick butter
1 1/2 cups granulated
cane sugar
1 1/2 cups pumpkin (not
pumpkin pie mix)
1/2 tsp vanilla bean paste
(or vanilla extract)
1 egg

Directions:

Preheat oven to 350°F.

Combine flour, baking soda, baking powder, cinnamon, nutmeg, ginger and salt in a bowl mix until combined. Set aside.

In another bowl, cream sugar and butter until blended. Add the pumpkin, egg, and vanilla paste.
Add flour mixture slowly to pumpkin mixture. Drop by tablespoon onto cookie sheet. Bake 8-10 minutes or until light brown.

**Frost or serve plain

SUGAR COOKIE CUT-OUTS
(Submitted by Pam Greenslate)

Ingredients:

1 1/2 cups powdered sugar
1 cup butter or margarine, softened
1 teaspoon vanilla
1/2 teaspoon almond extract
1 egg
2 1/2 cups Gold Medal™ all-purpose flour
1 teaspoon baking soda
1 teaspoon cream of tartar
Granulated sugar or colored sugar

Directions:

Mix powdered sugar, butter, vanilla, almond extract and egg in large bowl. Stir in remaining ingredients except granulated sugar. Cover and refrigerate at least 2 hours.

Heat oven to 375°F. Lightly grease cookie sheet.

Divide dough in half. Roll each half 1/4-inch-thick on lightly floured surface. Cut into desired shapes with 2- to 2 1/2-inch cookie cutters. Sprinkle with granulated sugar.

Place on cookie sheet. Bake 7 to 8 minutes or until edges are light brown. Remove from cookie sheet. Cool on wire rack.

FLOURLESS PEANUT BUTTER CHOCOLATE CHIP COOKIES
(Submitted by Catherine Ojalvo)

Makes about 24 cookies

Ingredients:

1 cup super-chunky peanut butter
1 cup(packed) golden brown sugar
1 large egg
1 tsp. baking soda
1 tsp. vanilla extract
1cup miniature semisweet chocolate chips (about 6oz.)

Directions:

Preheat oven to 350ºF.

Mix first 5 ingredients in medium bowl. Mix in chocolate chips. Using moistened hands to form generous 1tablespoon dough for each cookie. Arrange on 2 ungreased baking sheets, spacing 2 inches apart.

Bake cookies until puffed, golden on the bottom and still soft in the center, about 12 minutes. Cool on sheets for 5 minutes. Transfer to racks and cool completely.

SNOWBALL COOKIES
(Submitted by Keri Knutson)

Ingredients:

2 cups all-purpose flour
1/2 cup ground almonds
1/4 teaspoon salt
1 cup butter, softened (2 sticks)
1/2 cup powdered sugar
3 teaspoons water
1 teaspoon almond extract
36 maraschino cherries, rinsed and patted dry
1 cup powdered sugar
1 tablespoon milk
2 cups coconut flakes

Directions:

Preheat oven to 350°F.

Whisk together the flour, almonds, and salt.

In another mixing bowl, beat together butter and ½ cup sugar until light and creamy. Beat in the water and almond extract. Stir in the flour mixture until a dough forms.

Take tablespoons of dough and form a ball around each cherry. Place about 2 inches apart on baking sheets and bake for 18-20 minutes or until bottoms are browned. Remove to wire racks to cool completely.

To Glaze:

In a small bowl, mix a cup powdered sugar and 1 tablespoon milk. Dip the cooled cookies in the glaze and then roll in shredded coconut.

Makes 3 dozen cookies.

Grandma's Opera Fudge
(Submitted by Keri Knutson)

Ingredients:

2 cups sugar
1/2 cup milk
1/2 cup half-and-half
1 tablespoon light corn syrup
1/2 teaspoon salt
1 tablespoon butter
1 teaspoon vanilla
1/3 cup chopped candied red cherries

Directions:

Line a 5-3/4x3x2-inch loaf pan with foil or parchment paper and butter or spray with cooking spray.

In 2-quart saucepan, combine the sugar, milk, half-and-half, corn syrup and salt. Cook over medium heat, stirring constantly, until sugar dissolves and mixture comes to a boil. Keep boiling and stirring constantly until a candy thermometer reads 236°F (soft ball stage).

Remove saucepan from heat and add butter and vanilla. Cool at room temperature for 20 minutes, and then beat for five minutes. Stir in cherries. Pour into loaf pan and spread evenly. Place in refrigerator to cool. When chilled, remove fudge from pan and cut into pieces.

Makes 2 dozen pieces.

DUTCH SOUR CREAM COOKIES
(Submitted by Sherri Titus)

Ingredients:

1/2 cup soft butter (1 stick)
1 cup sugar
1 egg
1/2 teaspoon orange or lemon extract
1/2 teaspoon vanilla extract
3 cups all-purpose flour
1/4 teaspoon soda
1/4 cup sour cream

Directions:

Cream butter; gradually add sugar, beating until light and fluffy. Add egg and flavorings; beat well. Add flour, soda and sour cream.

Shape dough into a long roll, 2 inches in diameter; wrap in waxed paper, and chill 2 to 3 hours or until firm. Unwrap roll and cut into ¼ inch slices; place on ungreased cookie sheets.

Bake at 375°F for 8-10 minutes.

Yields 4 dozen

Soft Raisin Cookies

(Submitted by Sherri Titus)

Ingredients:

3 1/4 cups flour
3 eggs
1 1/2 cup sugar
1 cup soft butter or margarine
2 teaspoons grated lemon peel

1 teaspoon baking soda
1 teaspoon vanilla extract
1/2 teaspoon salt
1 1/2 cup dark seedless raisins
1 1/2 cup chopped walnuts

Directions:

Make early in day or up to 2 weeks before serving.

Into large bowl – measure all but raisins and nuts. With mixer at low speed, beat ingredients until just mixed. Increase speed to medium and beat 2 minutes, occasionally scraping bowl with rubber spatula. Stir in raisins and nuts until they are well blended.

Preheat oven to 375°F. Drop batter by heaping tablespoon about 2 inches apart on greased cookie sheet.

Bake 12-15 minutes until lightly browned around the edges. With pancake turner, remove cookies to wire rack to cool completely. Store cookies in tightly covered container.

Makes 2 1/2 dozen.

BLUEBERRY OATMEAL COOKIES
(Submitted by Sherri Titus)

Ingredients

1 package wild blueberry muffin mix
3/4 cup quick-cooking oats
1/4 cup brown sugar
1/2 cup cooking oil
1 tablespoon milk
1 egg

Directions

In a medium bowl combine all but the blueberries: mix well. Drop from a teaspoon onto an ungreased cookie sheet. Make a deep depression in the center of each cookie and fill with 7-8 well-drained blueberries. Push dough from sides to cover berries and pat down.

Bake at 375ºF for 8-10 minutes, until light brown.

RECIPES FROM *GINGERBREAD AT MOONGLOW*

Excerpt from *Gingerbread at Moonglow*

"Any idea how many people are participating in the cookie exchange?" Maisie asked.

"I'd say fifteen to twenty," Mist said. "All the regulars, plus a few new residents of Timberton. Betty made sure to let them know they were welcome."

Maisie nodded, placed the last dried dish in a cupboard and set the towel aside. "Well, I know Millie will be here. She stopped by the shop the other day to pick up a holly wreath, and said she'd be bringing Ginger Snaps – a special recipe from her grandmother.

"I'm not surprised," Mist said. "I suspect we'll have more ginger-related treats than other years. The gingerbread house seems to have inspired that theme."

"Don't worry," Maisie said. "There'll be all types of cookies. I heard Sally is bringing at least one variety of French macarons, Marge made 'Kitchen Sink Cookies' and Glenda's contributing vegan sugar cookies. The church guild ladies are bringing several batches of cookies, but didn't say what kind." She left to check the café, and returned to the kitchen. "Should I start setting everything up, maybe put out paper plates now, for people to fill with cookie assortments?"

"We're using baskets this year," Mist said, smiling.

"Baskets?" Maisie asked as Betty entered the room, back from the gallery.

"Yes," Betty said, jumping into the conversation. "Mist found some light balsa wood baskets, like berry baskets, but a little bigger. They're just the right size to hold a couple dozen cookies. I loved the idea of sending people home with something they can reuse. Mist even decorated them with her usual artistic flair."

"I simply painted a holly leaf on one side of each basket," Mist said. "We'll have clear cellophane and red organza ribbon, so they can be wrapped as gifts."

Gingerbread Cookies

(Submitted by Kim Davis, from her blog,
Cinnamon and Sugar and a Little Bit of Murder)

Ingredients:

8 ounces (2 sticks) unsalted butter, softened to room temperature
1 cup granulated sugar
2 large eggs
1/2 cup molasses
4 cups all-purpose flour
2 tablespoons cocoa powder
1 teaspoon salt
2 tablespoons ground ginger
1 tablespoon ground cinnamon
2 teaspoons cloves
1/2 teaspoon cayenne powder
1 teaspoon baking soda

Directions:

In a standing mixer beat butter and sugar together at medium speed until fluffy. Add the eggs, one at a time, and beat until thoroughly combined, then mix in molasses.

In a separate bowl, whisk together the flour, cocoa, salt, spices and baking soda, then slowly add to butter mixture, mixing on low speed until well combined.

Divide the dough into two portions and wrap well with plastic wrap. Refrigerate at least 8 hours or overnight.

On a lightly floured surface, roll the dough out 1/4 inch thick and cut out shapes using your favorite cookie cutters. Place on parchment lined baking sheets and bake at 350 degrees for 10 – 12 minutes or until lightly browned, rotating baking sheet half way through. Cool cookies on baking sheet for five minutes then finish cooling on a wire rack. Frost with your favorite icing and/or sprinkles.

CHERRY PECAN HOLIDAY COOKIES
(Submitted by Vera Kenyon)

Ingredients:

1/2 cup butter
1/2 cup margarine
1 cup powdered sugar
1 egg
1 teaspoon vanilla
2 1/4 cups flour

1 cup chopped pecans
4 or 6 ounces each: red and green candied cherries, chopped into four pieces (cutting with kitchen scissors works well)

Directions:

Using an electric mixer, cream butter, margarine, sugar, egg, and vanilla at medium speed until light and fluffy. At low speed, add flour. Stir in chopped pecans.

Divide dough in half; add red chopped cherries to one half, green cherries to the other half. Shape each half into a 2-inch-diameter log. Wrap in waxed paper and chill for 4 hours or overnight.

Preheat oven to 350 degrees. Cut logs into 1/4-inch slices; place 2 inches apart on ungreased cookie sheets.

Bake for 8-10 minutes, until light golden brown.

Makes 4 1/2 dozen cookies. The cookies freeze well, so they are great to make ahead.

GINGERBREAD-EGGNOG TRIFLE

(Submitted by Kim Davis, from her blog,
Cinnamon and Sugar and a Little Bit of Murder)

Ingredients:

1 (14.5 ounce) box gingerbread cake mix baked
according to the package directions*
1 (5.1 ounce) box instant vanilla pudding mix
3 cups eggnog (store bought and low-fat version is
fine) *Or use Homemade Eggnog recipe
1 tablespoon bourbon (optional)
2 (8 ounce) containers Cool Whip
Mini gingersnaps or gingerbread boy cookies for
garnish (optional)

Directions:

Bake the cake mix according to package instructions.
Cool completely before assembling the trifle.

Add pudding mix to a large bowl and whisk in the
eggnog and bourbon if using. Whisk for 2 minutes
until the mix is thoroughly smooth. Chill for at
least 30 minutes, or can be made up to 1 day in
advance.

Once the cake is cool, crumble half the gingerbread
into the bottom of a trifle or glass bowl.**
Spread half the pudding mixture over the cake, then
spread 1 container of Cool Whip over the pudding.

Repeat the layers with the remaining ingredients.

Chill at least 6 hours or overnight.

Garnish with mini gingersnap or gingerbread boy cookies as desired.

Tips:

*If you can't find a gingerbread cake mix, you can substitute a spice cake mix. Add 2 teaspoons ground ginger and replace 2 tablespoons of the vegetable oil called for in the mix with 2 tablespoons molasses. Bake as directed on package.

**You can also make individual servings using wine goblets or cocktail glasses.

HOMEMADE EGGNOG

(Submitted by Kim Davis, from her blog,
Cinnamon and Sugar and a Little Bit of Murder)

Ingredients:

3 cups whole or 2% milk (if you want to be extra decadent, use half and half)
4 eggs

1/2 cup granulated sugar
3/4 teaspoon vanilla
Pinch of salt
Dash of fresh grated nutmeg

Directions:

In a heavy saucepan, whisk the eggs, sugar, vanilla, salt and nutmeg together. Set aside.

In a microwave safe bowl, heat the milk in the microwave until hot. Don't boil. I use my 'beverage' button for this step.

Once the milk is hot, slowly add it to the egg mixture continually whisking to keep the eggs from overheating.

Place saucepan over medium-low heat on the stovetop and, whisking constantly, heat the mixture to 160 degrees (F). If you don't have a thermometer, the mixture should coat the back of a spoon, but for safety, use a thermometer.

Remove eggnog from heat and pour through a strainer. Completely chill the eggnog before using.

Cocoa Kisses

(Submitted by Peggy McAloon)

Ingredients:

3 egg whites
1 cup sugar
1/8 teaspoon salt
1 teaspoon vanilla
3 tablespoons cocoa
3/4 cup chopped nuts

Directions:

Beat egg whites to soft moist peaks; gradually beat in sugar and salt. Continue beating until mixture is thick and glossy; egg whites will stand in peaks.

Fold in vanilla, cocoa, and nuts.

Drop from a teaspoon onto buttered cookie sheet.

Bake in preheated very slow oven (250 degrees) for about 30 minutes or until kisses are partly dry and retain their shapes. Remove from pan while hot.

LOIS TALLMAN'S GINGER SNAPS

(Submitted by Deb Kenyon Thom)

Ingredients:

2 eggs
2 cups sugar
1 cup lard, melted
1 cup sorghum (or molasses)
1 teaspoon salt
1 tablespoon baking soda
1 tablespoon vinegar
2 tablespoons ground ginger
4 cups flour (plus more, if needed)

Directions:

Beat eggs, then add sugar, and beat again.

Dissolve soda in vinegar and add to mixture. Add sorghum (or molasses) and stir together.

Add salt and ginger in with flour, and mix together with other ingredients.

Roll the dough into balls the size of hulled walnuts.

Bake at 375 degrees for 10-12 minutes.
*More flour may be needed to make the dough sufficiently stiff.

Santa's Whiskers Cookies
(Submitted by Nettie Moore of Moore or Less
Cooking Blog)

Prep time: 20 mins
Cook time: 10 mins
Total time: 30 mins
Makes: 5 dozen

Delicious shortbread cookies filled with cherries,
wrapped in toasted coconut

Ingredients:

3/4 cup butter, softened
3/4 cups sugar
1 tablespoon milk
1 teaspoon vanilla
2 cups all-purpose flour
3/4 cup maraschino cherries, drained and finely
chopped
1/3 cup finely chopped pecans
3/4 cup coconut

Directions:

In a large mixing bowl, beat butter with an electric
mixer on medium to high speed for 30 seconds.

Add sugar and beat until combined. Keep scraping
sides of bowl.

Beat in milk and vanilla until combined.

Beat in flour on low, as long as you can.

Stir in the remaining flour.

Stir in cherries and pecans.

Shape dough into two 8 inch long rolls and roll in the coconut.

Wrap in plastic wrap and place in the refrigerator for 2-24 hours.

Cut into 1/4 inch thick slices and place 1 inch apart on to an ungreased cookie sheet.

Bake at 375 degrees for 10 to 12 minutes, until the edges are golden brown.

Transfer cookies to a wire rack to cool completely.

ANGEL CRISP COOKIES

(Submitted by Peggy McAloon)

Ingredients:

1/2 cup white sugar
1/2 cup brown sugar
1 teaspoon vanilla
2 cups flour
1 cup shortening
1 teaspoon soda
1 egg
1/2 teaspoon salt

Directions:

Combine all ingredients and roll into balls.

Dip half of the ball on the top side into cold water and then sugar.

Place sugar side up on cookie sheet.

Bake at 375 degrees 9-12 minutes.

Press down the center with a finger and add candied cherry or colored icing.

KOURABIEDES

(Submitted by Elizabeth Christy)

(Greek butter cakes)

Ingredients:

2 1/4 cups flour
1/2 pound margarine or butter
3/4 cup confectioners' sugar

3/4 tablespoon brandy
1/4 teaspoon almond extract
A pinch to 1/4 teaspoon ground cloves

Directions:

Cream together butter and sifted sugar up to 15 minutes.

Sift flour into mix gradually.
Add brandy, almond extract, and cloves and mix well.

Let dough stand in refrigerator for 30 minutes.

Shape into small diamonds about 2 inches by 1 1/2 inches.

Place on ungreased cookie sheets.
Bake at 350 degrees for 20 minutes or until cakes are sandy or light brown.

Cool and place in tin or plastic container.
Sift generously with confectioners' sugar.

Kitchen Sink Cookies

(Submitted by Cynthia Blain)

Prep: 20 minutes Total: 35 minutes, plus cooling
These cookies are chewy and rich, sweet and nutty.
Dried apricots or dates also work well. For a tropical
variation, substitute sweetened shredded coconut for
the oats. Keep up to 3 days in an airtight container at
room temperature. Makes 24.

Ingredients:

2 1/2 cups all-purpose flour (spooned and leveled)
1 teaspoon salt
1 teaspoon baking powder
1/2 teaspoon baking soda
1 cup (2 sticks) unsalted butter, room temperature
1 cup packed light-brown sugar
1 1/2 teaspoons light corn syrup
1 tablespoon pure vanilla extract
2 large eggs
1 cup semisweet chocolate chunks
1/2 cup raisins
1/2 cup chopped pecans
1/2 cup old-fashioned rolled oats (not quick-cooking)

Directions:

Preheat oven to 375 degrees. Line two large baking
sheets with parchment paper; set aside.

In a large bowl, whisk together flour, salt, baking powder, and baking soda; set aside.

Using an electric mixer, beat together butter, sugar, corn syrup, and vanilla until light and fluffy. Beat in eggs, one at a time, until well incorporated. Gradually beat flour mixture into butter mixture just until combined.

With a rubber spatula, fold in chocolate chunks, raisins, pecans, and oats.

Drop 2-inch balls of dough, spaced 2 inches apart, onto prepared baking sheets. Flatten dough balls slightly. Bake 12 to 16 minutes, or until cookies are lightly browned, rotating sheets halfway through.

Cool 5 minutes on sheets; transfer to a wire rack to cool completely.

Ginger Orange Cookies

(Submitted by Cynthia Blain)

This classic orange sable dough produces cookies with a remarkably delicate texture -- they crumble the minute they're in your mouth.

Ingredients:

Makes about 1 1/2 pounds.
1 1/4 cups whole blanched almonds
1 cup confectioners' sugar
3/4 cup (1 1/2 sticks) unsalted butter
3 tablespoons finely grated (2 to 3 oranges) orange zest
1 large egg
1 tablespoon freshly squeezed lemon juice
1 1/2 cups all-purpose flour
6 ounces crystallized ginger, finely chopped (about 1 cup)

Directions:

Place almonds and sugar in the bowl of a food processor. Process until the mixture resembles coarse cornmeal, and set aside.

Place butter and orange zest in the bowl of an electric mixer fitted with the paddle attachment. Beat on medium speed until white and fluffy, 2 to 3 minutes.

On low speed, add the almond mixture, and beat until combined, 10 to 15 seconds. Add egg and lemon juice, and combine. Add flour, and beat until combined.

Wrap in plastic; store, refrigerated, up to 1 week, or freeze up to 3 months. Chill this soft dough very well so it holds its shape when rolled in the ginger.

Place two 12-by-16-inch pieces of parchment on a work surface. Divide dough in half and form each half into a rough log on parchment. Fold parchment over dough; using a ruler, roll and press dough into a 1 1/2-inch cylinder. Wrap. Chill at least 3 hours.

Heat oven to 350 degrees.

Line two baking sheets with parchment. Spread crystallized ginger on a work surface. Unwrap logs; roll in ginger to coat. Cut logs into 1/4-inch-thick rounds and place on sheets, spaced 2 inches apart.

Bake until edges turn slightly golden, about 15 minutes. Transfer cookies to a wire rack to cool. Bake or freeze remaining dough. Store in an airtight container up to 2 weeks.

CHRISTMAS SWIRL FUDGE
(Submitted by Lenda Burns)

Prep: 10 Min.
Total time: 1 HR 10 Min.
Makes: 64

Ingredients:

1 bag (12 oz) white vanilla baking chips (2 cups)
1 container vanilla frosting
Green and red gel food colors

Directions:

Line 8-inch square pan with foil, leaving foil overhanging at 2 opposite sides of pan; spray foil with cooking spray.

In large microwavable bowl, microwave white chips uncovered on High 1 minute. Spoon frosting over chips. Microwave on High 30 seconds; stir. If necessary, continue to microwave in 15-second increments until mixture can be stirred smooth.

Place 3/4 cup fudge mixture into each of 2 small bowls, leaving remaining untinted fudge mixture in bowl. Tint 1 bowl green and 1 bowl red by stirring in each food color to desired color.

Drop heaping tablespoons of green, red and white fudge mixture in bottom of pan to create random pattern. Pull table knife through layers for marbled design. Refrigerate uncovered until set, about 1 hour.

Remove from pan by lifting foil; peel foil away. Cut into 8 rows by 8 rows. Store covered in refrigerator.

GRANDMA'S KRINGLES
(Submitted by Mary Brockhoff)

Ingredients:

1 lb. butter
1 egg
1 1/4 cups sugar
1 teaspoon almond extract
3 1/2 cups flour

Directions:

Work butter until creamy. Add beaten egg.

Add sugar, almond extract, and flour.

Mix and drop by spoonful on baking sheet. Bake at 500 degrees for a couple of minutes.

VEGAN SUGAR COOKIES
(Submitted by Megan Rivers)

Ingredients:

2 Tablespoons ground flaxseed
1/4 cup non-dairy milk (I used Almond Milk or Cashew Milk)
2 1/2 cup sugar
3/4 cup vegan butter (I use Earth Balance)
1 teaspoon vanilla extract
3 cups + 2 Tablespoons flour
2 teaspoons baking powder
1/2 teaspoon salt

Directions:

Mix the ground flaxseed and milk in a small bowl, set aside.

In a large mixing bowl, mix together the sugar and butter with a hand mixer until fluffy.

Add vanilla extract and the flaxseed/milk mixture to the bowl. Mix until blended.

Sift the flour, baking powder, and salt into the bowl and mix using a hand mixer until blended.

Roll the dough into a log-shape. Use parchment or wax paper to help the dough keep its shape and refrigerate for one hour. NOTE: You do not have to roll the dough into a log shape, but it is easier to work with.

Once refrigerated, cut dough into cookie sheets. Bake in the oven at 400 degrees for 5-7 minutes or until the edges are golden brown.

MINT CHOCOLATE MACARONS

(Submitted by Lisa Maliga, from her book, Baking French Macarons: A Beginner's Guide)

Macaron Shells

Ingredients:

100 grams almond flour
200 grams powdered sugar
3 large egg whites
50 grams finely granulated sugar
¼ teaspoon cream of tartar
1/2 teaspoon natural green powdered colorant

Temperature: 300 degrees Fahrenheit/150 Celsius

Directions:

Line 3 baking sheets with parchment paper or silpats. Double the baking sheets to prevent browning. Place a template on a baking sheet and put the silpat or parchment paper over it. You can have 3 different templates or just one, which you'll remove after piping each tray. Have a pastry/piping bag with a large round tip ready before you begin.

Sift powdered sugar with the almond flour. Whisk to make sure it's fully blended.

In a stainless steel or glass bowl, beat the egg whites at a low speed until foamy like a bubble bath before adding the cream of tartar. Then add granulated sugar in 3 batches. Increase the speed of your mixer. When finished, the mixture should have stiff peaks.

Add powdered colorant to the flour sugar mixture and then add half the flour/sugar mixture to the meringue. Fold until the mixture comes together, scraping the sides and flip batter over. The batter will be very thick. When the sugar/flour mixture is blended, the batter will be easier to mix and will look shiny. Lift the spatula and note if the batter falls in ribbons from the spatula. Another test is to write the number 8 with the batter.

Scoop batter into piping bag with your spatula. Twist the top of the bag and untwist the bottom, gently pushing the just-poured batter toward the bottom. This removes any excess air.

Pipe batter on the parchment or silpat-lined baking sheets in 1.5-inch circles. Keep the batter just inside circles if using a template.

Rap baking sheet several times on the counter. This will further flatten the macarons, and remove air bubbles. Place a towel on the counter to lessen the noise!

Preheat oven to 300 degrees Fahrenheit/150 Celsius.

Allow macarons to sit for 30-60 minutes until a film forms. Lightly touch a macaron shell and if no batter clings to your finger then it's dry and ready to be baked.

Bake for approximately 20 minutes. Use either the center rack or the one just below it. After about 10 minutes, rotate the tray. The tops should be firm and glossy and the bottoms of the shells should have formed feet or frills at the bottom. When done, the cookies can easily be removed from the parchment or silpat.

Remove from oven and gently slide the parchment or silpat onto a cooling rack. The shells should be cool enough to remove after 10 minutes.

Place macaron shells on a wax paper covered surface for filling. Match the closest sized shells together. For filling your macarons, use a piping bag and the tip size/style is your choice. Don't overfill the shells.

Chocolate Mint Ganache Filling

(Submitted by Lisa Maliga, from her book, Baking French Macarons: A Beginner's Guide)

Macaron Filling

Ingredients:

4 ounces heavy cream [120 grams]
4 ounces mint chocolate [120 grams]
1 teaspoon vanilla bean paste
½ teaspoon peppermint extract or a few drops peppermint essential oil

Directions:

Chop up the chocolate and place in a medium glass bowl. Put heavy cream in a glass container and set microwave timer for 50 seconds. It should be on the verge of boiling. Pour hot cream over chocolate chunks that are in a glass bowl. Whisk both ingredients together a few times. Add the vanilla bean paste and peppermint EO. Cover with cling wrap and let sit overnight. The next day, mix once more and spoon into a piping bag.

EASY COOKIES
(Submitted by Shelia Hall)

Ingredients:

1 box cake mix (any flavor)
1 box instant pudding mix (any flavor)
1 egg
1 cup oil

Directions:

Mix all ingredients together and roll into 1 inch balls.

Place 2" apart on a greased cookie sheet.

Bake at 325 degrees for 10 minutes or until golden brown.

KHRUSTYKY

(Submitted by Cynthia Blain)

Also called 'Ears', this Ukranian pastry is light and crunchy. Really easy to prepare, and makes a HUGE batch.

Ingredients:

2 eggs
3 egg yolks
2 tablespoons sugar
1 tablespoon rich cream
2 tablespoons rum or brandy (Or 1 teaspoon of rum, almond or pure vanilla flavoring)
1/2 teaspoon salt
1 cup plus 2 tablespoons sifted flour
Oil or shortening for deep frying

Directions:

Beat the eggs and egg yolks together until light in color.

Beat in sugar, rum or brandy (or extract), cream, and salt.

Stir in the flour. This dough should be soft. Cover and let rest for 10 minutes.

Roll out small amounts of dough at a time, with LOTS of flour on your rolling surface, put flour on top of the dough and on your rolling pin (this dough is very sticky otherwise). Roll to 1/8-inch or thinner. Keep the un-used dough covered to prevent drying out.

Cut the dough into long strips, about 1 1/4-inches wide. Then further cut the strips into 2 1/2 or 3-inch segments, diagonally (they will look like 2 1/2-inch long and 1 1/4-inch wide diamonds.) Make a slit in the center (about 1/2-inch long in the middle, lengthwise...) Grasp the bottom tail of the Khrustyky, put it through the slit in the middle, and pull it gently back down to the bottom (this will form a twist in the dough). Continue to do this to each piece of dough. (I roll out a small portion, cut and form my Khrustyky, and set them on a plate. Once my small bit of dough that I've rolled out is all used up, I fry these in the deep fryer before moving on to another piece of dough to roll and cut).

Deep-fry a few at a time in oil at 375 degrees F until light brown. These puff up as you fry them, making a delectable treat. Drain on paper towels. Sprinkle with confectioner's sugar.

Peanut Brittle
(Submitted by Olivine Kenyon)

*Pre-grease a cookie sheet

Ingredients:

1 cup sugar
1 cup raw peanuts
3/4 cup white Karo syrup
1/4 teaspoon salt
1 teaspoon baking soda

Directions:

Put sugar, syrup, and peanuts in pan, mix well and cook to a light golden color. Add salt and stir well.

Turn off burner, put in soda, stir about 15-25 seconds and dump quickly on well-greased cookie sheet.

Tip all corners of sheet and allow candy to spread all on its own. *This last process must be done very quickly!

Cool fast and eat. To break up bang cookie sheet on countertop!

SWEDISH COCONUT COOKIES
(Submitted by Nettie Moore)

Prep time: 35 mins
Cook time: 10 mins
Total time: 45 mins
Makes: 72 cookies

Ingredients:

3 1/2 cups flour
2 cups sugar
2 cups butter, softened
1 tablespoon baking powder

1 teaspoon baking soda
1 teaspoon vanilla
1 cup sweetened flaked coconut

Directions:

Combine all ingredients except coconut in large bowl.

Beat at low speed with a hand mixer, scraping bowl often, until well mixed.

Stir in coconut.

Divide dough in half; shape each half into a 12x2-inch log.

Wrap each log in plastic food wrap; refrigerate for at least 2 hours until firm.

Heat oven to 350°F.

Cut logs into 1/4-inch slices.

Place 2 inches apart onto parchment lined cookie sheets.

Bake 10-14 minutes or until edges are lightly browned.

Cool 1 minute on cookie sheet; remove to cooling rack.

RECIPES FROM *NUTCRACKER SWEETS* AT *MOONGLOW*

Excerpt from *Nutcracker Sweets at Moonglow*

In the short time Mist had spent with guests in the front parlor, a dozen additional townsfolk had shown up for the cookie exchange.

"Can you believe the variety this year?" Betty sidled over near Mist and offering her some mocha candied nuts. "Clayton's mother brought peanut brittle that cooks in a microwave. Imagine that! And I don't know how Maisie managed to pull off Minty Chocolate Macarons with little Clay Jr. crawling around, but she did."

"I may have gained five pounds just walking into this room," Mist said, eyeing a basket of assorted cookies on its way in.

"Marge brought wire baskets lined with parchment paper for everyone to fill," Betty said. "She's been using those for gift baskets this year. I've seen a few of them displayed in her store. It's nice she had enough to share with everyone here today."

"Christmas brings generosity out in people," Mist said. Seeing Betty's non-committal look, she whispered, "not always, I know, but often enough that we can believe in little miracles."

"You simply must try this," Maisie said, one arm securing Clay Jr. on her hip, the other balancing a chocolate-toffee concoction. "Millie's niece Kim brought it over. It's called Christmas Crack."

Betty and Mist both leaned forward to inspect the goods. "Looks like it would go well with a cup of tea later," Mist said. "Maybe you could hide a couple pieces in the kitchen?"

"And hide them well, where Clive won't find them" Betty added, laughing. "He'll be looking for sure."

CHRISTMAS CRACK
(Submitted by Kim McMahan Davis, from her blog, Cinnamon and Sugar and a Little Bit of Murder)

Ingredients

1-1/4 sleeves saltine crackers (about 50 crackers)
1 cup butter
1 cup brown sugar
1 (12-ounce) package chocolate chips (milk, semi-sweet, or dark)
1 (8-ounce) package toffee pieces

Instructions

Preheat oven to 400 degrees (F)

Line a baking sheet with foil.

Lay the saltine crackers on the baking sheet, arranging so no space remains between the crackers. It's okay to break the crackers into pieces to fit as needed.

Melt the butter in a medium-sized saucepan over medium heat then add the sugar and stir until it dissolves. Bring to a boil then reduce the heat to medium-low and boil for 4 minutes.

Immediately pour over the saltine crackers and using a spatula, make sure all the crackers are covered with the mixture.

Bake for 7 - 9 minutes, or until bubbly. Remove from the oven and sprinkle the chocolate chips over the top and return to the oven for 1 minute.

Remove from the oven and using a spatula, spread the chocolate over the tops of the crackers. Make sure the chocolate covers the entire surface.

Sprinkle the toffee pieces over the top of the melted chocolate.

Cool to room temperature for 30 minutes then place in the refrigerator for 30 - 60 minutes, or until the chocolate is firm.

Remove the Christmas Crack from the pan and break into pieces.

Store in an airtight container for up to two weeks.

WHITE CHRISTMAS FUDGE
(Submitted by Jean Daniel)

Ingredients:

2 1/2 cups granulated sugar
1/2 cup sour cream
1/4 cup milk
2 tablespoons butter
1 tablespoon light corn syrup
1/4 teaspoon salt
2 teaspoons vanilla
1 cup quartered candied cherries
1 cup chopped walnuts (could also use pecans)

Directions:

Combine sugar, sour cream, milk, butter, corn syrup and salt in heavy saucepan. Stir on moderate heat until the sugar completely dissolves, and mixture reaches boil.

Boil over medium heat 9-10 minutes or until it reaches 238 on candy thermometer. Remove from heat and allow to stand for an hour. It should reach at least 110 before you add the vanilla.

Beat until the mixture loses its gloss, which may take a little bit and some elbow grease but it will get there.

Stir in cherries and the nuts. Pat into a buttered pan. Cut into squares.

CATHEDRAL COOKIES

(Submitted by Teri Fish)

Ingredients:

½ cup butter
1 (16 ounce) package milk chocolate chips
1 teaspoon vanilla extract
1 cup chopped walnuts (optional)
1 (16 ounce) package colored miniature marshmallows
2 cups flaked coconut

Directions:

Melt butter and chocolate chips in heavy saucepan over medium heat; mix until smooth and creamy; remove from heat and stir in the vanilla. Fold in marshmallows and walnuts.

Scatter about half of the coconut onto a large baking sheet lined with wax paper. Pour the mixture into log on the coconut lined wax paper pour more coconut on top of it and with the wax paper roll the mixture into a log. Refrigerate until log is firm, about 1 hour.

Cut log into ¾ inch slices. Keep refrigerated to keep from melting.

Option: You can also microwave chocolate chips for 30 seconds on high then add butter and microwave in 30 second increments until smooth. Then add vanilla, marshmallows and nuts.

If you don't like or can't use coconut you can use powdered sugar. I have poured chocolate mixture onto wax paper rolled into log and then sprinkled powdered sugar over all sides.

MOLASSES SUGAR COOKIES
(Submitted by Bea Tackett)

Ingredients:

3/4 cup shortening
1 cup sugar
1/4 cup molasses
1 egg
2 teaspoon baking soda
2 cups flour
1/4 teaspoon cloves
1/2 teaspoon ginger
1 teaspoon cinnamon
1/2 teaspoon salt

Directions:

Melt shortening in a saucepan over low heat. Remove from heat; let cool.

Add sugar, molasses and egg; beat well.

Sift together flour, salt, and spices. Add to first mixture; mix well.
Form into 1" balls; roll in sugar and place on greased cookie sheet, 2" apart.

Bake at 375 degrees for 8-10 minutes.

Peanut Butter Fudge
(Submitted by Petrenia Snodgrass Etheridge)

Ingredients:

1 bag of peanut butter chips
1 tub of milk chocolate cake icing.

Directions:

Melt peanut butter chips in microwave or double boiler.

Gradually stir in icing and pour into 9x9 baking dish.

Allow to set for several hours and cut into squares.

Note: Use chocolate chips for regular fudge, or add pecans or walnuts for variety.

LEMON CRINKLES

(Submitted by Kim McMahan Davis, from her blog, Cinnamon and Sugar and a Little Bit of Murder)

Ingredients:

1/2 cup unsalted butter, room temperature
1 cup (7.1 ounces) granulated sugar
1 egg, room temperature
1/2 teaspoon vanilla extract
1/2 to 1 teaspoon lemon extract, depending on how lemony you want
1 teaspoon lemon zest
1 tablespoon fresh lemon juice
1-1/2 cups (7.2 ounces) all-purpose flour
1/2 teaspoon salt
1/4 teaspoon baking powder
1/4 teaspoon baking soda
1/2 cup granulated sugar (for rolling dough)

Directions:

Don't preheat the oven yet. The cookie dough will need to chill first.

Line baking sheet with parchment paper and set aside. In a medium-sized bowl, whisk together the flour, salt, baking powder, and baking soda. Set aside.

In the bowl of a standing mixer, whip the butter and granulated sugar together until fluffy, about 2 minutes on medium speed.

Add the egg and beat until fully incorporated.

Mix in the vanilla, lemon extract, lemon zest, and lemon juice.
With the mixer running on lowest speed, slowly add the flour mixture. Beat just until it is fully incorporated.

Cover the cookie dough with plastic wrap and allow to chill in the refrigerator for 1 hour or even overnight.

Preheat oven to 350 degrees (F).

Place remaining 1/2 cup granulated sugar in a shallow bowl.

Form cookie dough into small balls, about a heaping teaspoon.

Roll the balls in the granulated sugar and place on the parchment-lined baking sheet, at least 2 inches apart. Don't crowd the cookies as they spread. You should have 12 cookies per baking sheet.

Bake for 9 to 11 minutes. The edges should just be turning light golden and the tops should be crackled.

Remove from the oven and allow to cool on the baking sheet for 5 minutes before transferring to a wire cooling rack.

Cool completely and store leftovers in an airtight container at room temperature for up to 3 days.

Notes:

These cookies are ideal for making ahead of time and freezing for spur-of-the-moment freshly-baked cookies! Simply roll the dough balls in the sugar, then freeze them on a parchment-lined baking sheet. When solid, transfer the dough to a freezer-safe ziplock bag. When ready to bake, place the dough on a parchment-lined baking sheet and allow to sit at room temperature while pre-heating the oven. You may need to bake an additional minute, depending on how chilled the dough is when you start baking.

Makes 30 - 40 cookies depending on size.

Krum Kake Cookies
(Submitted by Lynette Ausland Eads)

Ingredients:

1 cup sugar
½ cup melted butter (or oleo)
½ teaspoon vanilla flavoring
3 eggs
½ cup whipping cream
2 cups flour
1 teaspoon nutmeg
½ to 1 teaspoon cardamom

Directions:

Beat cream and set aside. Beat eggs until very light, then add sugar, spices, melted butter, cream, & flavoring. May add almond or lemon flavoring instead of vanilla. Stir in flour.

Heat Krumkake iron on medium heat on stove top. Put a teaspoonful of batter on the iron. Close the iron, and bake one minute or less, turn iron over and bake until lightly browned. Remove cookie from iron and quickly roll on cone – shape form. Store in air tight container.

Notes:

Enjoy plain or filled with whipped cream.

CRANBERRY DROP COOKIES
(Submitted by Jan Knight)

Ingredients:

1/2 cup butter, softened
1 cup sugar
3/4 cup brown sugar
1/4 cup milk
2 tablespoons orange juice plus the zest of 1 orange
2 1/3 cup flour
1 teaspoon baking powder
1/4 teaspoon baking soda
1/2 teaspoon salt
1 cup chopped walnuts
2 1/2 cups coarsely chopped cranberries

Directions:

Wash cranberries in sieve. Drain on paper towels.

Cream butter & sugars. Beat in milk, orange juice, & egg.

Blend dry ingredients with whisk in a separate bowl. Add to mixture. Stir in nuts, cranberries, & orange zest.

Drop by teaspoonful onto nonstick baking sheet or parchment paper.

Bake at 350 degrees for approximately 12 minutes or until light brown. Let cool.

Option: Finish with a powdered sugar glaze tinted pink for a festive touch! Keep in a single layer in storage container.

DOUBLE CHOCOLATE WALNUT BROWNIES
(Submitted by Valerie Peterson)

Ingredients:

1 cup butter or margarine
4 sq. unsweetened chocolate
2 cups sugar
3 eggs
1 teaspoon vanilla
1 cup sifted flour
1 ½ cups coarsely chopped walnuts
1 package chocolate chips

Directions:

Melt butter and chocolate together.

Stir in sugar, eggs, and vanilla.

Add flour and mix well.

Pour into greased 9 x 13 pan.

Sprinkle with nuts and chocolate chips

Bake at 350 degrees for 35minutes.

GRANNY'S BUTTER ROLLS

(Submitted by Petrenia Snodgrass Etheridge)

Ingredients:

2 cups sugar
3 cups milk
2 teaspoons vanilla
2 cups flour
1 cup shortening
2/3 cup milk
1 or 2 sticks margarine

Directions:

Mix 3 cups milk, vanilla, and sugar and bring to a boil.

Knead flour and enough milk and shortening to make dough, as if making biscuits.

Roll out dough on cooking sheet or foil until it's thin.

Spread margarine with knife all over dough and sprinkle with sugar.

Roll dough up into a roll and cut in about 2-inch pieces.

Drop in milk mixture in deep casserole dish.

Bake at 350 degrees until rolls are brown.

CHRISTMAS HARD CANDY
(Submitted by Betty Escobar)

Ingredients:

3 ½ cups sugar
1 cup light corn syrup
1 cup water
¼ - ½ teaspoon cinnamon or peppermint oil
1 teaspoon red or green food coloring

Directions:

In a large heavy saucepan, combine sugar, corn syrup and water.

Cook on medium-high heat until candy thermometer reaches 300 degrees (hard-crack stage,) stirring occasionally.

Remove from the heat. Stir in oil and food coloring, keeping away from face, as odor is very strong.

Immediately pour onto a greased cookie sheet. Cool and break into pieces. Store in airtight containers.

Lingonberry Macarons

(Submitted by Lisa Maliga, from her book, Baking Macarons: The Swiss Meringue Method)

Ingredients:

160 grams powdered sugar, sift with almond flour
160 grams almond flour, sift with powdered sugar
150 grams egg whites
180 grams confectioners' sugar, sieved
1 tablespoon [8 grams] arrowroot powder
1/2 teaspoon [3 grams] cream of tartar
Purple or pink food gel color

Directions:

Preheat oven to 300 Fahrenheit/150 Celsius.

Sift the almond flour and confectioners' sugar together into a bowl. Stir in the arrowroot powder and set aside.

Put a template on a baking sheet and place a silicone mat or parchment paper over it. Set aside.

In the bowl of a stand mixer, add egg whites and confectioners' sugar. Whisk until well combined. Place bowl over steaming pot with just enough water, as you don't want the water touching the bowl. Heat on medium heat until it steams. Test to make sure it's hot enough by sticking your clean finger in the meringue near the center of the bowl. If using a candy thermometer the temperature should be about 130 F [54 C]. Remove from heat and place bowl back onto stand mixer.

Add the cream of tartar. Whisk on medium to high speed until firm peaks form. Egg whites should be glossy and if you flip the bowl upside down, nothing will come out.

Add food coloring and whisk until the color is incorporated.
Remove the whisk and add the paddle attachment [if using one].

Add the presifted almond flour and confectioners' sugar mixture.
Turn mixer to low or medium speed and mix for up to 10 seconds. If that doesn't mix the batter thoroughly, mix for another 10 seconds. Turn off mixer and with your spatula, run it around the sides and bottom of bowl to make sure all the dry ingredients are incorporated. Test for the ribbon stage. When you lift your spatula above the bowl, the batter should fall back to the bowl as one continuous stream and create a ribbon pattern.

Pour batter into a large pastry bag fitted with a large round tip. Pipe onto the silicone or parchment covered baking sheets. When finished with each sheet, bang baking sheet on counter to remove air bubbles. If you see any air bubbles, pop them with a toothpick.

Let shells rest on a flat surface in a cool, dry area for about 30 minutes. The surface will change from glossy to matte. To make sure they're done, gently touch the edge of one with your finger. There should be no trace of batter on your finger.

Bake for 15-20 minutes. This will vary depending on your oven. Carefully monitor the baking process and check your oven thermometer. After 8 or so minutes, rotate the tray to ensure even baking.

Macarons are done when you peel back the mat or the parchment paper and the shells don't stick.

Remove from oven and gently slide the parchment or silicone mat onto a cooling rack. The shells should be cool enough to remove after 10 minutes.

Place macaron shells on a wax paper covered baking sheet or tray for filling. Match similar sized shells together. Pipe the filling on the flat side of one shell and gently place the second shell on top.

Notes:

Lingonberries are tart like cranberries. They make a lovely contrast to sweet macaron shells.

LINGONBERRY BUTTERCREAM FILLING

(Submitted by Lisa Maliga, from her book, Baking Macarons: The Swiss Meringue Method)

Ingredients:

Lingonberry jam, strained
220 grams [2 cups] confectioners' sugar, sifted
1 teaspoon vanilla
Burgundy gel food colorant

Directions:

Add the butter to the bowl of a stand mixer and mix until creamy.

Add the strained lingonberry jam, followed by the confectioners' sugar.

Mix on high speed for several minutes.

Spoon into a piping bag with a round or star-shaped tip.

YUMMY DATES
(Submitted by Deb Kenyon Thom)

Ingredients:

Large fresh dates
English walnuts
Powdered sugar

Directions:

Slice open a large fresh date and remove the seed.

Insert half of an English walnut.

Pinch date closed and roll in powdered sugar.

TWENTY-FIRST CENTURY PEANUT BRITTLE
(Submitted by Deb Kenyon Thom)

.

Ingredients:

1 cup white sugar	1 teaspoon butter
1/2 cup light corn syrup	1 teaspoon vanilla
1 cup raw peanuts	1 teaspoon baking soda
1/2 teaspoon salt	

Directions:

Grease a large cookie sheet.

Using a large microwaveable bowl, mix sugar and syrup together. Heat in a microwave oven on high for three minutes.

Add peanuts and salt, stir then heat in a microwave oven for three more minutes.

Add butter and vanilla, stir and heat in a microwave oven for two or three minutes.

Remove from the microwave, add baking soda and stir well. It will get foamy. Immediately pour onto your buttered cookie sheet pan and spread it out with your spoon.

Let the candy cool and whack on the counter top or sturdy table to release candy from the pan.

Healthy No-Bake Apple Energy Bites

(Submitted by Lori Sparks Shoemake, from her blog 50 with Flair: www.50withflair.com)

Ingredients:

1-1/2 cups quick or old-fashioned oats (not instant)
3/4 cup creamy peanut butter, I use a natural type
3/4 cup grated apple
1/2 cup chopped pecans (or your choice of chopped nut)
1/3 cup ground flax seed (or flax seed meal)
1/3 cup honey
2 tablespoons sesame seeds (or your choice of small seeds)
1/2 teaspoon vanilla extract
1/2 teaspoon cinnamon (or ginger for some "bite", or cinnamon-ginger combination)

Directions:

Stir all ingredients together in a bowl until completely combined; extra oats can be added if the mixture seems too soft and sticky. Cover and chill in refrigerator for 30 minutes until firm. Then roll the mixture into 1-inch balls which should yield 18-20 bites. Store in an airtight container in the refrigerator for up to one week, if they last that long! Enjoy!

Tip: dampening your fingers/hands with a bit of water will keep the mixture from sticking to your hands too much

Notes:

45 minutes total time is 15 minutes prep, plus 30 minutes of chill time for the bites to firm up.

Try adding your favorite nuts, dried fruits or even protein powder, etc.

Grandma Chauncey's Date Nut Bars

(Submitted by Taryn Lee)

Ingredients:

1/4 cup oil
1 cup brown sugar
2 eggs
1/2 teaspoon vanilla
1/4 teaspoon ginger
3/4 cup flour
1/2 cup chopped pecans or walnuts
1 cup finely, chopped dates
Powdered sugar (to roll bars in)

Directions:

Mix oil and brown sugar. Add eggs and vanilla; beat well.

Add all dry ingredients except powdered sugar and stir well.

Put mixture into oiled 8X8 inch pan.

Bake at 350 degrees for 30 to 35 minutes.

Cut into bars and roll in powdered sugar.

No-Bake Peanut Butter Oatmeal Cookies
(Submitted by Betty Escobar)

Ingredients:

2 cups sugar
1/2 cup milk
4 tablespoons cocoa
3/4 stick butter
½ cup peanut butter
2 cups quick oats

Directions:

Bring to rolling boil and cook for 1 minute.

Take off heat and add 1/2 cup peanut butter and 1 teaspoon vanilla.

Stir until peanut butter is mixed in well, and then add 2 cups quick oats.

Form into balls or cookies of desired shape.

Cinnamon Refrigerator Cookies
(Submitted by Robyn Seitzer)

Ingredients:

3 ½ cups flour
1 teaspoon baking soda
1 tablespoon cinnamon
¼ teaspoon salt
1 cup shortening
1 cup brown sugar
1 cup white sugar
2 eggs
1 cup chopped nuts or raisins (optional)

Directions:

Combine flour, soda, cinnamon and salt. Set aside.

Cream shortening and sugars. Beat eggs until light then mix with creamed mixture.

Add dry ingredients 1/3rd at a time, beating after each addition. Add optional ingredients if desired.

Divide dough into two and roll into log until about two inches in diameter. Loosely wrap in waxed paper and refrigerate approx. one hour.

Pre-heat oven to 350. Slice and bake 7 to 10 minutes.

MOCHA CANDIED NUTS

(Submitted by Kathleen Brown)

Ingredients:

1-1/2 cups sugar (beet)
1 tablespoon corn syrup
1/2 cup warm, strong coffee (or 1 tablespoon instant coffee + 1/2 cup water)
2-1/2 cups walnuts, pecans, or other nuts

Directions:

Blend together in a saucepan the sugar, corn syrup, and coffee.

Cook to softball stage (240 degrees Fahrenheit,) about 4 minutes.

Remove from heat and add the nuts. Stir until creamy.

Turn onto a greased cookie sheet or waxed paper; separate nuts with 2 forks. Let cool.

All-In-One-Pan Cookies

(Submitted by Kathleen Brown)

Ingredients:

1/2 cup butter or margarine
1 cup crushed graham crackers
1 cup coconut
1 cup chocolate chips
1 cup chopped nuts
1 can (14 oz.) sweetened condensed milk

Directions:

Melt butter in 9" x 13" pan.

Add graham crackers to butter.

Sprinkle on coconut, chocolate chips, and nuts.

Drizzle on sweetened condensed milk.

Bake at 350 degrees for 20-25 minutes. Cut into squares.

DATE BALLS
(Submitted by Vera Kenyon)

Ingredients:

8 oz. package of dates, chopped
2 eggs, lightly beaten
1 stick of butter
1 cup of chopped nuts
2 teaspoons of vanilla
2 cups of crispy rice cereal
2+ cups of flaked, sweetened coconut (for rolling the date balls)

Directions:

Melt the butter over low heat. Don't let it get too hot.

Whisk in the dates, eggs and vanilla. Stir well. Cook for approximately five minutes.

Add in the nuts and crispy rice cereal. Mix well.

While the mixture is still warm form into small balls and then roll in coconut. Work fast. Let cool.

Freezes well so you can make these up ahead of the holiday.

RECIPES FROM
SNOWFALL AT
MOONGLOW

Excerpt from *Snowfall at Moonglow*

"And to think that it started with a plate of cookies," Betty said as she stood next to Mist. "Well, I'll clarify that. Technically, it started as a flirtation at their church. But I bet those cookies she took him from the cookie exchange a few years ago didn't hurt."

"Now that you mention it," Mist said, "do you need help preparing for the event tomorrow? It seems more people join in every year, although I know you always have everything under control." The traditional cookie exchange had been established long before Mist came to Timberton.

Betty tapped Mist's arm in a gesture of appreciation. "Marge and Millie will both be here early. I imagine we can handle it even if we get some unexpected participants."

"I made several extra papier-mâché baskets in case more people show up than you expect," Mist said. "I'll have them all on the kitchen counter for you to distribute as needed."

"Maybe you can help by keeping Clive out of the room," Betty said, laughing.

"I heard that," Clive said as he passed by with more firewood.

"Add Clayton to that list!" Maisie had just approached, carrying a sleepy Clay Jr. in her arms. "I'm heading home. It's time to put this little guy to bed. Plus Clayton's parents arrive on Christmas Eve day, so I only have tomorrow to get ready for their visit. I'll be at the cookie exchange though. I wouldn't miss it."

"Did I hear something about cookies?" Andrew said.

Betty laughed. "Don't worry. We always make a large plate for guests. You'll find the assorted goodies in the lobby tomorrow evening."

Peanut Butter Cookies
*gluten-free and low-carb
(Submitted by Petrenia Etheridge)

Ingredients:

1 cup peanut butter
1 cup coconut sugar
1 egg
1 teaspoon vanilla

Directions:

Mix ingredients together well.

Using a teaspoon, spoon onto a cookie sheet about 2-3 inches apart.

Press with a fork that was dipped in water.

Bake at 350 degrees for 8-10 minutes.

Cool on rack and enjoy.

**Note: Holds shape better after a few hours of cooling.

NORWEGIAN KRINGLA
(Submitted by Jan Knight)

Ingredients:

1 cup sugar
1/2 cup butter, softened
1 egg
1/2 teaspoon salt
1/2 teaspoon vanilla
1 cup buttermilk
1 teaspoon baking soda
3 1/2 cups flour
1 teaspoon baking powder (Stir into flour)

Directions:

Beat sugar and softened butter together.
Beat in eggs, salt and vanilla.

Mix together flour and baking powder. Set aside.

Whisk baking soda into buttermilk.

Add flour/ baking powder mixture and buttermilk/ baking soda mixture alternately into the butter mixture until well mixed. It will be very stiff and slightly sticky to the touch.

Cover and chill in the refrigerator for 24 hours or overnight.

Take a small amount of dough out of the refrigerator at a time, as it will be hard to work with if it gets soft. By heaping teaspoon, roll into a ball with your fingers first, and then roll to a pencil-sized round strip on a floured pastry cloth/board.

Shape into a pretzel by crisscrossing the strip and flipping one end through the middle.

Put on parchment-lined baking sheets. Form all the kringla before putting them in oven to ease your preparation process.

Bake at 350 degrees about 10 minutes or more until bottoms are just golden and top is just set. Do not overbake! Watch closely, as oven temps and baking time may vary.

JO'S FUDGE
(Submitted by Betty Escobar)

Ingredients:

2 cups sugar
½ cup milk
½ cup corn syrup
¼ cup cocoa
¼ cup butter
1 teaspoon vanilla

Directions:

Butter an 8 x 8 x 2 pan.

Mix sugar, milk, corn syrup, and cocoa in a medium sauce pan and cook on low heat to a soft boil, only stirring occasionally.

Add butter and vanilla and cook an additional 5-10 minutes. Pour into pan and let set.

**Optional: Add nuts or coconut.

WUNDERBAR GINGER BAR COOKIES

(Submitted by Robyn Seitzer)

Ingredients:

2 1/4 cups flour
1/2 teaspoon baking soda
1/4 teaspoon salt
1/2 teaspoon ginger
1/2 teaspoon cinnamon
1/4 teaspoon ground cloves
1/3 cup margarine
2/3 cup dark brown sugar, packed
1/2 cup dark molasses
1/2 cup water
1/2 cup raisins or nuts

Glaze:

1 cup powdered sugar
2 tablespoons hot water

Directions:

Preheat oven to 375. Grease a jelly roll pan.

Sift together dry ingredients and set aside.

Cream margarine and sugar with electric mixer. When light and fluffy, add in molasses.

Add dry ingredients alternately with water, beginning and ending with dry ingredients, beating well between additions.

Fold in raisin or nuts and spread into pan.
Bake 15 to 20 minutes. Cool in pan.

Glaze by mixing powdered sugar with hot water. Spread over cake. Cut into 2 1/2 inch by 1 1/4 inch bars. Store in a tightly closed container.

Orange Sablés

(Submitted by Kim Davis, from her blog,
Cinnamon and Sugar and a Little Bit of Murder)

Originating in France, Sablés are a shortbread-style
cookie with a buttery, melt-in-your-mouth texture.
With the addition of colored sanding sugar, these
refreshing orange cookies are perfect for any holiday.

Ingredients:

1-1/2 cups all-purpose flour
3/4 cup cornstarch
1 cup unsalted butter, room temperature
3/4 cup confectioners' sugar
1/2 teaspoon salt
1 tablespoon orange zest
1 teaspoon vanilla extract
1/2 teaspoon orange extract
1 cup colored sanding sugar

Directions:

Beat the butter in the bowl of an electric mixer set on
medium speed until creamy.
Turn mixer to low and slowly add the confectioners'
sugar and beat until incorporated.

Slowly add the cornstarch, flour, and salt to the sugar
mixture. Beat just until combined.

Add the orange zest, vanilla extract, and orange extract
and mix on low until well combined.

Divide the dough in half and roll each portion into logs, about 10 inches long.

Spread the sanding sugar onto a flat plate and roll each log in the sugar, pressing to adhere it to the dough.

Wrap each log in plastic and chill at least 8 hours or overnight.
Preheat oven to 350 degrees (F) and line baking sheets with parchment paper.
Remove the plastic wrap from the dough logs, and slice into 1/4-inch slices. Place on prepared baking sheets at least an inch apart.

Bake 10 to 15 minutes. You don't want these to brown, but pale golden on the bottom is fine.

Allow the cookies to cool on the baking sheet for 5 minutes, then transfer to a wire rack to cool completely.

Tips:

**If dough is too difficult to slice through after being refrigerated, allow to sit at room temperature for 15 minutes to soften.

**Use different colored sanding sugars on each log for holiday celebrations, such as red and green for Christmas; pink and red for Valentine's; red and blue for Independence Day; etc.

**To make ahead of time, once the dough has been wrapped tightly in plastic, you can freeze the logs in heavy-duty freezer ziplock bags for up to 2 months. Allow to defrost in the refrigerator overnight then proceed with slicing and baking as per instructions.

LEMON NUT COOKIES
(Submitted by Jean Daniel)

Ingredients:

1 cup shortening
1/2 cup sugar
1/2 cup brown sugar
1 egg beaten well
1 tablespoon of grated lemon rind
2 tablespoons lemon juice

1/4 teaspoon soda
2 cups sifted all-purpose flour
1/4 teaspoon salt
1/2 cup chopped nuts
*good with walnuts, pecans, almonds

Directions:

Cream shortening until light and fluffy, add the sugars gradually.
Add the egg, lemon juice, and the rind. Mix well.

Add the sifted dry ingredients a little at a time until mixed well. Add nuts.

Make into a roll about 2 inches round. Wrap in wax paper and chill for at least an hour.

Cut 1/4 inch thick slices, place on greased cookie sheet.

Bake at 325 degrees for just shy of 15 minutes.

CINNAMON COOKIES
(Submitted by Jean Daniel)

Ingredients:

1 cup sugar
1/2 cup shortening
1 egg
1/4 cup milk
1/2 teaspoon salt
2 cups flour
2 teaspoons baking powder
1 1/2 tablespoons cinnamon

Directions:

Cream sugar and shortening until soft. Add well-beaten egg to the milk.

Sift flour with baking powder, salt, and cinnamon. Add alternately with liquid to the sugar mix.

Drop by spoonful on greased tin.

Bake at 400 for 20 minutes. *Can be iced after they cool.

CHOCOLATE PEPPERMINT BARK
(Submitted by Faith Creech)

Ingredients:

12 oz. white chocolate
12 oz. dark chocolate
1/2 cup crushed candy canes

Directions:

Line a 9 x 12 pan with parchment paper.

Place dark chocolate in a glass bowl and melt in microwave.

Pour onto parchment paper and use a spatula to spread.

Melt the white chocolate the same way and spread over the dark chocolate, spreading evenly.

Crush candy canes. Sprinkle on top of white chocolate while still hot.

Let harden in the refrigerator for two hours. Then break into pieces.

Mrs. Prager's Cry Babies

(Submitted by Wendy Matchett)

Ingredients:

1 cup shortening
1 cup sugar
1 egg, beaten
1 cup molasses
1/2 cup hot water
1/2 teaspoon ginger

1 teaspoon cinnamon
1/2 teaspoon cloves
1/2 teaspoon nutmeg
5 cups flour
2 teaspoons baking soda
1 teaspoon salt

Frosting:

1 tablespoon butter or margarine
2 tablespoons strong coffee, hot
1 teaspoon vanilla
1-1/2 cups sifted confectioners' sugar

Directions:

Cream shortening and sugar together.
Add 1 egg, beaten.
Add molasses and all spices.

Sift together flour, baking soda, and salt. Add to mixture.

Drop by teaspoon on cookie sheet.
Bake at 400 degrees for 12-15 minutes.

Mix frosting ingredients and frost while hot.

CHOCO-MINT PUFFS
(Submitted by Jan Knight)

Ingredients:

2 egg whites
2/3 cup sugar
Pinch of salt
1/4 teaspoon green food coloring
1/8 teaspoon mint flavoring
6-8 oz. miniature chocolate chips

Directions:

Preheat oven to 400 degrees. Cover cookie sheet with parchment paper.

Whip egg whites to soft peaks. Add sugar gradually. Add a pinch of salt & beat until stiff.

Fold in food coloring, mint flavoring, and miniature chocolate chips.

Drop by teaspoon on parchment-lined pans. Place in hot oven & then turn off the oven immediately. Do not open door until the next morning.

Store in an airtight container. Makes 2 dozen.

**Alternate method: Bake at 275 degrees for 20 minutes. Turn oven off; leave in oven with door ajar for 30 minutes. Cool. Peel off paper.

Pecan Pie Cobbler

(Submitted by Taryn Lee)

Ingredients:

6 tablespoons butter
1 cup whole pecans
1-1/2 cups self-rising flour
1-1/2 cups granulated sugar
2/3 cups milk
1 teaspoon vanilla
1-1/2 cups light brown sugar, packed
1-1/2 cups hot water

Directions:

Preheat oven to 350 degrees.

Add butter to 9x13 casserole dish and melt in oven. Once butter is melted, sprinkle pecans over butter.

In bowl, mix flour, sugar, milk, and vanilla. Stir to combine. Don't over mix.

Pour batter over butter and pecans. Don't mix.

Sprinkle brown sugar evenly over batter. Don't mix.

Carefully and slowly pour hot water over the mixture. Don't mix.

Bake 30 to 35 minutes or until golden brown.

MERINGUE CHOCOLATE-CHIP COOKIES

(Submitted by Sue Powers Hampshire) (makes
4 dozen)

Ingredients:

4 egg whites at room temperature (cannot be
purchased in a carton at the grocery store) - cannot
have a drop of egg yolk or whites will not rise)
2 cups of sugar
12 oz. bag of chocolate chips

Directions:

Preheat oven to 400 degrees.

Whip egg whites on highest speed until peaks are
formed.

Gradually add sugar to mixture while still mixing.

Fold in chocolate chips.

Using small spoons, place dropfuls of cookie dough
on ungreased cookie sheet.

Put cookie sheets into oven and turn off the oven.

Keep cookie sheets in oven overnight or for several
daytime hours.

EVE'S APPLE PECAN POUND CAKE
(Submitted by Angela Sanford)

Ingredients:

3 cups all-purpose flour
1 teaspoon baking soda
1 teaspoon salt
2 cups sugar
1-1/2 cups of vegetable oil
3 large eggs - room temperature
2 teaspoons of vanilla extract
3 cups of apples (peeled, cored, and chopped) *granny smith apples recommended
1 cup pecans, toasted and chopped
1 cup sweetened, shredded coconut

Directions:

Preheat oven to 325 degrees. Grease and flour a 10-cup tube pan.
In a large bowl, combine flour, salt, and baking soda. Set aside.
Combine oil, sugar, eggs, and vanilla extract in a large mixing bowl.

Mix at medium speed until well blended.

Using low speed, mix in apples, coconut, and pecans.

Spoon batter into the prepared pan.

Bake for 80 minutes or until a toothpick inserted in center comes out clean. **Do not open oven during baking.

On a wire rack, cool in pan for 10 minutes. Invert onto rack to cool completely.

*Option – Add Homemade Caramel Sauce:

HOMEMADE CARAMEL SAUCE
(Submitted by Angela Sanford)

Ingredients:

1 cup packed brown sugar
1/2 cup of butter
1/4 cup of milk
1 teaspoon vanilla extract

Directions:

Bring sugar, butter, and milk to a gentle boil. Cook until thickened, usually 1-2 minutes.

Remove from heat and stir in vanilla extract. Drizzle on cake.

PUMPKIN COOKIES
(Submitted by Micki Kremenak Jordan)

Ingredients:

1 cup sugar
1/2 cup butter, softened
1 egg
1 cup pumpkin
1 teaspoon vanilla
2 cups flour
1 teaspoon soda
1 teaspoon baking powder
1 teaspoon cinnamon
1 cup chopped dates

Directions:

Mix sugar and butter.

Mix in egg, pumpkin, and vanilla.

Mix together flour, soda, baking powder, and cinnamon. Add to mixture.

Stir in dates.

Drop cookies on parchment covered cookie sheet and bake 10 minutes at 350 degrees.

Cool and frost with powdered-sugar frosting.

Polka Dots

(Submitted by Shelia Hall)

Ingredients:

1 (21oz) box fudge brownie mix
1/2 cup oil
2 eggs, slightly beaten
1 cup white chocolate chips

Directions:

Combine the brownie mix, oil, and eggs. Stir well.

Stir in chips and drop by rounded teaspoons 2 inches apart on greased cookie sheet.

Bake at 325F for 8-10 minutes.

Let cool before removing from pan.

PFEFFERNÜSSE FRUITCAKE COOKIES
(Submitted by Dawn Moore)

Ingredients:

1/2 cup sugar
1/2 cup shortening
1/2 cup dark corn syrup
1/2 cup coffee
3-1/4 cups flour
1-1/2 teaspoons baking soda
1/2 teaspoon cinnamon
1/4 teaspoon salt
1/4 teaspoon nutmeg
1/2 cup candied cherries
1/2 cup raisins
1/2 cup dates
1/2 cup walnuts
2 eggs
1 teaspoon anise seed
1-1/2 teaspoons lemon extract

Directions:

Combine sugar, shortening, corn syrup, and coffee in a 3-quart saucepan. Simmer 5 min. and cool.

Sift together flour, baking soda, cinnamon, salt, and nutmeg. Set aside.

Grind candied cherries, raisins, dates, and walnuts. Set aside.

Add eggs, anise seed, and lemon extract to shortening mixture. Mix well.

Stir in the dry ingredients and then the fruit mixture. Blend well and chill at least 4 hours or overnight.

Shape into 1" balls with well-floured hands and place on greased cookie sheet.

Bake at 350 degrees for 15-18 min. Dip warm cookies into glaze and place on racks to set. Store in a tightly covered container.

**Sugar Glaze: Combine 1 cup sugar, 1/2 cup water, and 1/4 teaspoon cream of tartar in a small saucepan. Boil until clear. Cool. Stir in 1/2 cup sifted powdered sugar.

CHOCOLATE REFRIGERATOR COOKIES
(Submitted by Micki Kremenak Jordan)

Ingredients:

1-1/4 cups butter, softened
1-1/2 cups confectioners' sugar
1 egg
1-1/4 teaspoons salt
3 cups cake flour
1/2 cup cocoa
1-1/2 cups chopped pecans *May be added to cookies rather than on outside.
4 oz. sweet chocolate

Directions:

Cream butter and sugar until light and fluffy.

Add egg and mix well. Whisk together salt, flour, and cocoa. Add to mixture and blend well.

Chill dough for about an hour to make easier to handle.

Mold into rolls and then roll in nuts. Wrap in wax paper and refrigerate overnight.

Slice 1/8" thick and bake on ungreased cookie sheet. Bake in 400-degree oven about 10 minutes. Cool.

Melt chocolate and frost center of cookies.

PECAN DREAMS

(Submitted by Cecile VanTyne)

Ingredients:

2 sticks unsalted butter, room temperature
2 cups all-purpose flour
4 tablespoons granulated sugar
2 teaspoons pure vanilla extract
1 cup finely chopped pecans
1 to 1-1/2 cups powdered sugar for coating the cookies

Directions:

Preheat oven to 300 degrees
Add the butter and sugar to the bowl of a stand mixer or use a hand mixer. Mix on medium speed until combined, then mix on high speed until very light and creamy, about one minute.

Add the vanilla and mix to incorporate. Add the flour and pecans and mix just until the flour is incorporated.

Using a small cookie scoop, place a scoop of cookie dough in your hand and roll it into a ball, then place the ball onto a large, ungreased cookie sheet. Repeat until all of the dough is rolled into balls.

Bake for 30 minutes or until the cookies are just lightly browned on the bottoms. Remove from the oven.

Allow the cookies to cool for 2 to 3 minutes, then roll the cookies, one at a time, in the powdered sugar and transfer to a piece of waxed paper.

Once the cookies have completely cooled, reroll the cookies one more time in the powdered sugar. If you like a generous coating, you might need more powdered sugar.
Store cookies in an airtight container using waxed paper to separate the layers.

Aunt Shirley's Oatmeal Cookies

(Submitted by Nana Fields)

Ingredients:

1 cup of raisins
3/4 cup of hand broken chunks of walnuts
Boiling water
1/4 cup of reserved liquid from drained raisins (a little more if desired)
1 small bowl to put raisins and boiling water in
3 cups of oats, instant or regular
1 cup of flour
1 teaspoon of salt
1/2 teaspoon of baking soda
3/4 cup of shortening
1 egg
2 teaspoons of real vanilla extract
1 cup of firmly packed brown sugar
1/2 cup of granulated sugar

Directions:

Preheat oven to 350 degrees.

Grease cookie sheet or use parchment paper; set aside.

Put raisins in small bowl and cover with boiling water; let stand for 5 minutes, then drain. Reserve drained liquid from raisins for later use.

In a bowl, mix together oats, flour, salt and baking soda. Set aside.

In a large bowl, beat together brown sugar, granulated sugar, egg, 1/4 cup of reserved liquid drained from raisins, vanilla until very creamy. May do by hand or use a mixer.
Slowly stir in dry ingredients until thoroughly mixed. Stir in raisins and nuts until evenly mixed.

Drop mounded teaspoonfuls onto prepared cookie sheet and bake for about 12 to 15 minutes or until done but still soft. Don't overbake.

Let stand for 2 minutes and transfer cookies to wire cooling rack. Ovens may vary so check on cookies the first time you make them.

Lone Ranger Cookies
(Submitted by Cinda Unruh)

Ingredients:

2 cups flour
1 teaspoon baking powder
1 teaspoon baking soda
1/2 teaspoon salt
1 cup shortening
1 cup sugar
1 cup packed brown sugar

1 teaspoon vanilla
3 eggs
3/4 cup wheat germ
3/4 cup cornflakes
1-3/4 cups crispy rice cereal
1-3/4 cups oatmeal

Directions:

Sift together flour, baking powder, baking soda, and salt. Set aside.

Mix together shortening, sugar, and brown sugar. Add vanilla and eggs.

Add flour mixture and then mix in wheat germ, cornflakes, crispy rice cereal and oatmeal.

Drop by rounded spoonful on a greased cookie sheet.

Bake at 350° for 12-15 minutes.

Mystery Bars

(Submitted by Micki Kremenak Jordan)

Ingredients:

2 cups finely crushed graham crackers
1/2 cup coarsely-chopped pitted dates
1/2 cup coarsely-chopped pecans
1/2 cup semisweet chocolate chips
1 cup sweetened condensed milk

Directions:

Preheat oven to 350 degrees.

Spray either 8x8x2 or 9x9x2 pan.

Combine all ingredients and mix evenly. Spoon mixture into pan.

Bake about 30 minutes. Cool in pan on wire rack.

Cut into bars.

**Alternate combinations:

*Use 1/2 cup chopped marshmallows instead of dates.

*Leave out chocolate chips and increase dates and pecans to total of 1-1/2 cups.

RECIPE NOTES

RECIPE NOTES

RECIPE NOTES

RECIPE NOTES

Other Titles by Deborah Garner

Mistletoe at Moonglow

The small town of Timberton, Montana, hasn't been the same since resident chef and artist, Mist, arrived, bringing a unique new age flavor to the old western town. When guests check in for the holidays, they bring along worries, fears and broken hearts, unaware that Mist has a way of working magic in people's lives. One thing is certain: no matter how cold winter's grip is on each guest, no one leaves Timberton without a warmer heart.

Silver Bells at Moonglow

Christmas brings an eclectic gathering of visitors and locals to the Timberton Hotel each year, guaranteeing an eventful season. Add in a hint of romance, and there's more than snow in the air around the small Montana town. When the last note of Christmas carols has faded away, the soft whisper of silver bells from the front door's wreath will usher guests and townsfolk back into the world with hope for the coming year.

Gingerbread at Moonglow

The Timberton Hotel boasts an ambiance of near-magical proportions during the Christmas season. As the aromas of ginger, cinnamon, nutmeg and molasses mix with heartfelt camaraderie and sweet romance, holiday guests share reflections on family, friendship, and life. Will decorating the outside of a gingerbread house prove easier than deciding what goes inside?

Nutcracker Sweets at Moonglow

When a nearby theatre burns down just before Christmas, cast members of The Nutcracker arrive at the Timberton Hotel with only a sliver of holiday joy. Camaraderie, compassion, and shared inspiration combine to help at least one hidden dream come true. As with every Christmas season, this year's guests will face the New Year with a renewed sense of hope.

Snowfall at Moonglow

As holiday guests arrive at the Timberton Hotel with hopes of a white Christmas, unseasonably warm weather hints at a less-than-wintery wonderland. But whether the snow falls or not, one thing is certain: with resident artist and chef, Mist, around, there's bound to be a little magic. No one ever leaves Timberton without renewed hope for the future.

Above the Bridge

When NY reporter Paige MacKenzie arrives in Jackson Hole, it's not long before her instincts tell her there's more than a basic story to be found in the popular, northwestern Wyoming mountain area. A chance encounter with attractive cowboy Jake Norris soon has Paige chasing a legend of buried treasure, passed down through generations. Side-stepping a few shady characters who are also searching for the same hidden reward, she will have to decide who is trustworthy and who is not.

The Moonglow Café

The discovery of an old diary inside the wall of the historic hotel soon sends NY reporter Paige MacKenzie into the underworld of art and deception. Each of the town's residents holds a key to untangling more than one long-buried secret, from the hippie chick owner of a new age café to the mute homeless man in the town park. As the worlds of western art and sapphire mining collide, Paige finds herself juggling research, romance and danger.

Three Silver Doves

The New Mexico resort of Agua Encantada seems a perfect

destination for reporter Paige MacKenzie to combine work with well-deserved rest and relaxation. But when suspicious jewelry shows up on another guest, and the town's storyteller goes missing, Paige's R&R is soon redefined as restlessness and risk. Will an unexpected overnight trip to Tierra Roja Casino lead her to the answers she seeks, or are darker secrets lurking along the way?

Hutchins Creek Cache

When a mysterious 1920's coin is discovered behind the Hutchins Creek Railroad Museum in Colorado, Paige MacKenzie starts digging into four generations of Hutchins family history, with a little help from the Denver Mint. As legends of steam engines and coin mintage mingle, will Paige discover the true origin of the coin, or will she find herself riding the rails dangerously close to more than one long-hidden town secret?

Crazy Fox Ranch

As Paige MacKenzie returns to Jackson Hole, she has only two things on her mind: enjoy life with Wyoming's breathtaking Grand Tetons as the backdrop, and spend more time with handsome cowboy Jake Norris as he prepares to open his guest ranch. But when a stranger's odd behavior leads her to research western filming in the area - in particular, the movie, Shane, will it simply lead to a freelance article for the Manhattan Post, or will it lead to a dangerous hidden secret?

A Flair for Chardonnay

When flamboyant senior sleuth Sadie Kramer learns the owner of her favorite chocolate shop is in trouble, she heads for the California wine country with a tote-bagged Yorkie and a slew of questions. The fourth generation Tremiato Winery promises answers, but not before a dead body turns up at the vintners' scheduled Harvest Festival. As Sadie juggles truffles, tips and turmoil, she'll need to sort the grapes from the wrath in order to find the identity of the killer.

A Flair for Drama

When a former schoolmate invites Sadie Kramer to a theatre production, she jumps at the excuse to visit the Monterey Bay area for a weekend. Plenty of action is expected on stage, but when the show's leading lady turns up dead, Sadie finds herself faced with more than one drama to follow. With both cast members and production crew as potential suspects, will Sadie and her sidekick Yorkie, Coco, be able to solve the case?

A Flair for Beignets

With fabulous music, exquisite cuisine, and rich culture, how could a week in New Orleans be anything less than fantastic for Sadie Kramer and her sidekick Yorkie, Coco? And it is - until a customer at a popular patisserie drops dead face-first in a raspberry-almond tart. A competitive bakery, a newly-formed friendship, and even her hotel's luxurious accommodations offer possible suspects. As Sadie sorts through a gumbo of interconnected characters, will she discover who the killer is, or will the killer discover her first?

A Flair for Truffles

Sadie Kramer's friendly offer to deliver three boxes of gourmet Valentines truffles for her neighbor's chocolate shop backfires when she arrives to find the intended recipient deceased. Even more intriguing is the fact that the elegant heart-shaped gifts were ordered by three different men. With the help of one detective and the hindrance of another, Sadie will search San Francisco for clues. But will she find out "whodunit" before the killer finds a way to stop her?

A Flair for Flip-Flops

When the body of a heartthrob celebrity washes up on the beach outside Sadie Kramer's luxury hotel suite, her fun-in-the-sun soon turns into sleuthing-with-the-stars. The resort's wine and appetizer gatherings, suspicious guest behavior, and casual strolls along the beach boardwalk may provide clues, but will they be enough to discover who the killer is, or will mystery and mayhem leave a Hollywood scandal unsolved?

Cranberry Bluff

Molly Elliott's quiet life is disrupted when routine errands land her in the middle of a bank robbery. Accused and cleared of the crime, she flees both media attention and mysterious, threatening notes, to run a bed and breakfast on the Northern California coast. Her new beginning is peaceful until five guests show up at the inn, each with a hidden agenda. As true motives become apparent, will Molly's past come back to haunt her, or will she finally be able to leave it behind?